C000099302

More Friends T[...]

A Journey into Mediumship

Lynn Quigley

First Published and Printed in the UK

More Friends Than You Know

A Journey Into Mediumship

Lynn Quigley

Published by
J & L Quigley
P.O Box 122
Penmaenmawr
LL30 9AJ
UK

Copyright © 2007 by: Lynn Quigley

First Edition, 2007
ISBN 978-0-9534946-3-7

Published and Printed in the UK

I dedicate this book to:

My Mum and Dad – Dinah & Eric

and

My In Laws – Elsie & John

Epigraph

I recognise now, that all through my life, profound and poignant happenings and meetings have usually been marked with the receiving of an object, a keep-sake, the energy of the happening or meeting being held within it, in the same way as a precious crystal holds within it's form, energy, knowledge and it's own unique healing power.

(extract from Chapter Two)

Lying in bed that same night, I was suddenly aware that a man in a dark suit was standing very close to my side of the bed – just standing staring at me – saying nothing.
I dived under the bed covers and said the only thing that I knew to say – "Go to the light – Go to the light".
I lay and listened. Hearing nothing – I peeped out from under the covers to see if he had gone.
No – he was still there.
I dived again – "Go to the light, Go to the light" I implored.
Once more I peered out from my refuge – he was still there! – still standing, still saying nothing.

(extract from Chapter Eight)

Contents

Foreword

On very rare occasions we may meet someone – a unique individual – someone who has a profound impact on our lives and the way in which we see and interact with the world around us – Lynn Quigley is just such a person

I first met Lynn (Lynn Jenkins as she was then) in the late Summer of 1968. She was then, as she is now the most honest, direct, thoughtful and intuitive person I have ever known

In "More Friends Than You Know," Lynn writes about being aware of and communicating with spirit since her very early childhood. And for reasons she will explain, decided in early '91 to work more consciously and develop her communication skills in an expanded way in order to share with others the messages and teachings she receives from spirit

Lynn has always helped people with her natural intuitive counselling skills but from '91 onwards this became much more - consciously spirit led.

Refusing to compromise the integrity of her channelling Lynn has never (apart from a short time, sitting in circle) been on a workshop, course or training retreat to develop her ability, instead she has listened to her guides and friends in spirit, listened and acted upon their guidance, working closely with them to develop a mutual respect, trust and understanding which facilitates a deep and profound level of communication

Throughout this book you will find many references to spirit guides and guidance, as well as fascinating transcripts of wisdom and wit taken from channelled sessions that were part of Lynn's "mediumship training" by those in spirit

Parallel to and interspersed with this, is the story of a young girl growing up with all the joy, happiness, heartache and pain that physical life brings

Lynn writes as she lives her life – from the heart – in her usual open, refreshingly honest and down to earth manner – she tells it, "as it is" with, compassion, integrity and lots of humour

In reading "More Friends Than You Know" you will learn a little about Lynn the person and Lynn the medium (although the join is seamless) but more importantly you'll learn about the method which spirit used in training her to work the way she does, getting the amazing communication she gets without any fuss, ritual or drama.

If by now you are beginning to feel a degree of bias in my words, you are of course correct – Lynn and I have been together since our first meeting in the 60's and from that first meeting she has inspired and amazed me on a daily basis with her insight, understanding, love and compassion. Her intuition, wisdom and guidance has helped us, and many others, through good times and challenging times alike.

Read the book yourself and be inspired.

John Quigley

Preface

Hello.

Since 1994, when a Spirit guide gave me the title for this book – and told me that one-day I would write it – I have felt haunted by the prospect.

As the years went by – I quietly continued on my path of communication, spirit release and earth healing - trained by my Spirit guides (as I am still in training).

Trained, by them, in a no nonsense – step by step way.

I have never been on a course, and I have not read books on the subject – other than the books of Doris Stokes.

My husband John, is my earthly guide.

In many respects, my work with spirit leads me to live a solitary life.

I work "at a distance" with the spirit release and earth healing, and, generally speaking, work with individuals over the telephone and "at a distance".

This is how I have been trained to work.

One day, as I was on the telephone talking to a young lady called Maxine (who was, by now, working with a former guide of mine) she suddenly said: "He is mentioning a book – are you writing a book? – That's a good idea – you should write one".

I had started to write the book in 1998 – as he well knew! And the computer had EATEN IT!

An act, that left me devastated and even more determined to ignore these "subtle" hints and reminders.

I always knew that I would eventually, write this book – but - "Well – there's always tomorrow – isn't there?"

Another "hint" came, as; in response to the question from a friend called Hugh: "How did you start to work with Spirit?" I began to tell him about one or two of my experiences.
"You must write about them" he said, "It might help someone who is going through the same thing".

The final "nudge" came one day about 3 months before I began to write this book:
John had been working on his computer, and he came into the living room, carrying some A4 printed sheets.
"I found this," he said – handing me the sheets. "I've printed them off for you".
I looked down, to see a copy of my first attempt of "More Friends Than You Know".
John had tried long and hard to retrieve my book after it had disappeared, searching through all the back up discs – but to no avail. Now all these years later – the first attempt had revealed itself – with more than a little help, we suspect, from our "friends".

After reading those printed words, I said to John; "Well, no wonder it was lost – I had started in the wrong place".
From then on – the need to write this book became – ever urgent.
And so my tomorrow came, and I have now written this part of my story.

I must stress, that this is NOT a training manual, but a true and honest account of what happened to me.
I know that it will help someone.

I know that it will answer some questions – I also know that it will raise a few questions.

I have met, and continue to meet and work with - wonderful and amazing Spirits.
They continue to help many people and lost Spirits – unconditionally.
They continue to help me – unconditionally.

My personal reason, for writing this book - is that - I Love Them – I Respect and Trust Them - They can make me Laugh and Cry - and I wanted to share all that.

I also wanted to share with you the direct communications' I have received from them and this book has allowed me to do that.

Many Thanks.

Lynn.

Acknowledgements

I would like to thank EVERYONE whose name appears in this book, for the part you have played, in my life.

To those in Spirit, one of whom gave me the title for this book, I thank you for your eternal patience, guidance and teaching, sense of compassion, and humour.

I would especially like to mention my husband – John. Without whose encouragement, support, patience and considerable computer skills – this book would still be a twinkle in my guides' eye.

My Love & Thanks to you.

CHAPTER ONE

MY STORY BEGINS.

I announced my arrival into this life on the 4th December 1952, at 1pm.

A "home birth", as many were in those days, it was unclear if I would survive, as I had turned in the womb a few times – the consequence being that I was born with the umbilical cord wrapped around my neck, Having starved myself of oxygen, I was born a "black baby", with ginger hair.

Not a very encouraging start, and not a pretty sight!

However mum and the midwife decided to offer me up to the family pet – a Scottish Terrier called Laddie – who was given the job of cleaning me up, and with his help – I turned pink.

Of course with hindsight you can see the benefits of stimulating my system by the action of a dog's tongue on my body, similar to dogs and their puppies, and ewes with their lambs, but dogs have been known to kill the runt of the litter as well!

Fortunately for me, the latter was not his intent.

We've all heard of Tarzan and the Apes and Wolf Man, how about Canine Girl, and, on reflection, does the above event, bear any relevance to the fact that I went through a phase of nibbling dog biscuits, or is that completely normal childish behaviour?

I don't remember Laddie, but I have a photograph of him, taken with my mum and elder sister, and I use this opportunity to thank him publicly for all his efforts towards my survival. Thank you Laddie.

My arrival had been long awaited. Mum had had at least one miscarriage, (I was later to meet a sibling that had grown up in the Spirit world}, since the birth of my sister - hence the five-year age gap between my sister and I. Not long after my birth, my sister was allowed into the bedroom to view the new arrival, and asked, "Can we keep her?" My survival wasn't assured at that time, and given that I did, I'm sure that over the years, my sister has asked the question "Why did we keep her?" Particularly in my early school days, when she was given the responsibility of dragging me, kicking and screaming, on and off two buses, in order to get me to school. She was only 11yrs old at the time.

So here I was, ready to begin on this life's journey.

My family consisted of Mum and Dad, my sister, my paternal grandmother and my paternal grandfather. I was three weeks old, that Christmas, and my grandfather, whose name was John, but who was called Jack – bought me my first teddy bear. Sadly, granddad Jack died suddenly, when I was thirteen months old, but I do have a memory of standing, clutching onto his trouser leg, as he sat in a chair and smiling down at me.
There were also two aunts, one uncle and two cousins. All other members of the family were once or twice removed, or else had died.
Throughout my life, there were also a succession of dogs - four being the greatest number, at any one time.

I can't begin to imagine the pain – both physical and emotional – that Mum and Dad, particularly my Mum, of course, went through, to bring me into this world. I know that Dad wanted a boy and had chosen the name Glyn for him, but hey – they persevered and got me, and I very quickly made my presence felt.

By the time I was 11 months old, I was walking and talking incessantly. One of those toddlers that was into everything and always getting dirty. Legend has it - that I was dressed as I was going out of the door in my mums' desperate bid to keep me looking presentable.

Wilful and determined and insistent on pushing my trolley to the shops rather than sit in it and, apparently, I always had to stop and say "hello" to everyone that I met along the way.

Even at a few months old I would attempt to climb out of my pram - fighting against the restraints of the straps.

Mum would tell the story; how one day, when I was about nine months old, she placed my pram - with me in it - for a sleep in the front room. Returning some time later to check on me, she peered round the door and was met with the sight of a laughing, grinning, me, dangling - feet first - outside the pram, with just the pram straps keeping me from falling onto the floor.

Many, many years later, as I was talking to Spirit one day, I went into a spontaneous regression.

I saw myself, at about nine months old, in the front room of our house. I was hanging half in and half out of my pram. I, and my uncle Armon, were laughing because we could hear mummy coming. She opened the door, gasped, and ran towards me, her arms outstretched – a look of horror on her face.

What mum didn't realise, was that uncle Armon and Granddad (her brother and father who were both in Spirit) would never let me harm myself - we played together a lot.

I was also fascinated by the coal fire.

The fireguard was no barrier to me and Mum realised that teaching me how to poke the fire and put small pieces of coal onto it safely, was the easier and safer route to take. So it was that when I was around 2 yrs old, mum left me in the care of Auntie Batty. Auntie Batty was my name for Mr Batty, and he was a family friend and a painter and decorator, he had come to decorate the front room. While mum went to the shops, she left me with him (you can only imagine her relief of the chance to go to the shops without me in tow).

Anyway, legend has it that Aunty Batty left me in one room for a couple of minutes, and when he returned he found me poking the fire.

At this point in the story Mum would always smile as she recalled the look of panic that she saw on Aunty Batties face, when she returned home.

Apparently his first words were;

"Why didn't you warn me?"

"About what?" mum asked, (probably with an innocent look on her face).

"About Lynn – I only left her for a few minutes – and she was playing with the fire!"

Apparently, mum went on to explain that she had taught me how to poke the fire safely, adding that she was sorry for not warning him.

I suspect that the apology was more than a little "tongue in cheek".

Aunty Batty had had a fright, and apparently had spent the entire time she was away, watching my every move. As there are no other stories of when he looked after me, I assume he refused to!

Of course, young children managing open fires, is nothing extraordinary, you see it in many places throughout the world, but all the same, you can't help having a little bit of sympathy for Aunty Batty!

The area where I was born, and spent the first six years of my life, was full of family history.

An urban area - just on the outskirts of Northwich, Cheshire - where my mother and her two brothers had been brought up, and where my maternal grandparents and great grandparents (my great grandparents weren't blood family, but Mum always referred to them, as my great grandparents) had lived.

I knew the house where mum had lived, I knew the streets where granddad had sold coal from his horse and cart, and I knew that the black upright piano in the front room had to be treated with respect. Mum's brother Armon had played it, as he had also played the organ at the Zionist chapel. Armon was the reason why mum got upset on Christmas Eve, as it had been on Christmas Eve in 1946, that she and the family had heard the sad news that Armon, who had been imprisoned in a Japanese prisoner of war camp, had died.

I had no trouble at all in respecting and loving that piano and learnt to play it myself - in particular - a piece of music entitled "Melodie d' Amour" by H Engelmann. A piece of music that requires the full stretch of the hands, and the arms to cross over – a piece that Armon had played.

I always knew if Armon was with me when I played it, because I didn't seem to make as many mistakes and I sometimes used to wonder if Mum had noticed this phenomena as well, but I never dared to ask, I just hoped that she had; and that she knew that Armon was near.

So it was that I grew up in a house where possessions were treasured and respected, a way of holding on to the memory of their previous owners and users, a way of being near to them - bringing them, near to you. This is where I learnt to hold onto my toys and books so that they would become tools – tools used to trigger happy memories – too precious to give away. I know that memories are in your head, and that they stay with you but I have always liked to touch and hold my memories.

Of course you can't hold on to everything, nor would you wish to, and so it's then, that you have to rely on your memory:

Like the memory of my much treasured pram – a present when I was five or six. I loved that pram, I remember how it felt and smelt. I remember the joy of pushing my dolls proudly. I remember how the black bodywork and chrome handles and wheels shone in the sunlight after I polished it. I remember, when I was 21yrs old, deciding that I should "let it go". I remember believing the man who came to take it away, when he said it would go to a good home, but I have to admit that I have often wondered if it did.

So I have happy memories of my first home:

I remember the ICI train line, which ran past the bottom of the garden – and the train drivers who would wave to me as they trundled past.

I remember the excitement I felt, on the day a steam engine arrived to lay the tarmac road and I remember Mum, holding my sister over the hot tarmac, in the hope that the fumes would abate the cough she had – as a result of contacting whooping cough.

I remember walking to school on wet winter days – and the smell and feel of my wet gabardine mac.

I remember my black shiny Wellingtons, which allowed me to jump in puddles.

I am reminded of the "nature table" that was in our classroom, every time I smell chrysanthemums.

And – I remember the day my sister and her friend persuaded me to put on a pair of roller skates and encouraged me to hurtle down our driveway towards the two wrought iron gates. I remember how hard they laughed – as they opened the gates, just before I arrived - and hurtled onto the pavement and into the gutter.

Fortunately, for me, I don't remember the headmistress of my first school – who, apparently, did not like the way I always asked questions – who said that I was noisy, disruptive and didn't listen – and continually compared me to my sister - who was quiet and studious. "She will never be like her sister", was her criticism.

Mum simply pointed out to her that – I wasn't my sister – I was a different person and if she couldn't see that, then, that was her failing.

When my sister finished at that primary school at the age of eleven – we were both sent to another school and although, initially, I created a fuss - much to the annoyance of my sister – I learnt to love my new school.

When I was 6yrs old, we moved to a village a few miles away.

This was the first time I had moved house and everything about it was very exciting.
I remember being taken to see the house and being shown around it by the lady who lived there.
I remember standing in a bedroom, complete with wallpaper depicting circus activities, chosen by her, for her two boys. She seemed to be very proud of that wallpaper.

"I'm having this room", I blurted out, much to the embarrassment of my mother.

I was quickly reminded of my manners;

A. Do not interrupt adults when they are talking!

B. It is VERY rude to talk about who would have which room, whilst the lady was standing in front of you! (I got the impression that when you were going to move house, it was manners to pretend to the people who lived in that house, that you weren't actually going to live there, even though you were – if you "catch my drift"). It was all very confusing!

C. This was an occasion when children, especially me – "should be seen and not heard".

I thought the lady would like to know that I liked the wallpaper, I thought I was being polite – I could have mentioned the bars on the low window and how her explanation of them – "as a child safety measure" - could only mean that her two boys were sissies!

So it was one Easter that Mum and Dad, my sister, me and Lassie and Moss – our two dogs – moved into a house that had once been a rectory.

I took up residence in that bedroom with its circus wallpaper, and Dad quickly removed the bars from the window – to my great satisfaction.

Having a bedroom of my own gave me a wonderful feeling of privacy, and I revelled in the fact that I had my own personal space. Previously, my sister and I had shared a room, and I well remember how she would repeatedly switch the light on, by means of a long pull cord, which dangled over the bed. The clunk of the switch made me jump, and my frustration at not being able to reach the cord, in order to "get my own back", had been immense.

My new bedroom had two large wall to ceiling cupboards and I shared this storage space with Mum and Dad.

One possession of theirs, that was kept in the bottom of one cupboard, was a fragile Union Jack flag, which had been firmly attached to a garden cane, by the means of drawing pins. When I asked Mum about this flag, she told me that it had been made to hang out of the bedroom window of my Grandparents house – in celebration of V.E. day.

I can only imagine the feelings' of joy and relief that she felt on that day - and her excitement and expectation, that my father and her two brothers would soon be safe and back at home.

Sometimes, I would get the flag out and unfurl it – give it a few quick "waves" and then carefully roll it up again.

Living in an "ex" rectory (the proper one was located further down the street) meant that our house was occasionally mistaken for the "real" one. Imagine my confusion therefore, as a child, when, on answering the knock on the front door, on more than one occasion, I was asked by the couple who were standing there, if my dad could marry them.

This house was right next door to a parish church, which had a steeple. The steeple could be seen for several miles around and whenever we were travelling home from an outing, Dad would say, "You always know you are home, when you see the steeple". He was right; no matter how near or far we had travelled, the steeple was always waiting - to welcome us back.

The church also had a graveyard, and many a time I would wander around, looking at the many different headstones, and reading the inscriptions, always taking care not to walk on the graves, but always around them, as mum had told me.

There were weddings and funerals to watch, (as long as I kept out of sight of course). I achieved this, by positioning myself on the path that ran parallel to our garden. The path was edged with a stone wall, behind which, I crouched and crept – popping my head up and down quickly, in order to get a better view.

The large wooden doors to the entrance of the church, were always closed at the beginning of each service - by the verger or his wife - but even those mighty doors, could not completely prohibit the sound of the organ – and the singing – filtering through – if I listened very hard.

The verger and his wife lived in our street, and the sight of one or both of them, walking towards the church – their long black robes, billowing and sweeping behind them – was my early warning system – a service was going to take place.

The weddings, of course were more colourful than the funerals – made more so by the paper confetti that the guests would throw over the bride and groom.

I knew, (the verger had told my Mum, and she had told me) that - "It is against the rules, to throw confetti, within the church boundary!"

Oh! - How worried I was, on behalf of those guests who flouted that law. The sight of that confetti, swirling around the church doors – everyone laughing and joking – resulted in me, (in my safe haven, behind the wall) chewing my knuckles – in anticipation of "The Vergers Return!"

After the funerals, when everyone had gone, I would go and look at the flowers.
I would sometimes feel the sighs of relief made by some of the people who had been buried, as their family and friends left the church, many of them in tears – leaving the buried person, if I understood the sighs correctly, to relax, and giving Them a chance to look at the flowers and read the inscriptions' on the little cards.
The graveyard was always a peaceful place to be, a happy place, after all the people had gone of course.

And so I went through life always knowing that "they" were watching, sometimes, on reflection, hoping that they weren't, very often not thinking anything at all about them, only being reminded every so often by the smell of perfume, tobacco smoke or the occasional draught
The only death I had experienced so far in the family, that I remember, were the death of an uncle (several times removed) My only memory of that illness and subsequent death was, having been taken to a hospital car park to wait outside with my sister, a conversation of the adults when they emerged from visiting him, saying that he was "too weak to turn the pages of his book", and that he had to wait until a nurse came to turn the page over for him.
I has this mental image of him, sitting up in bed holding his book with both hands, like I did, and reading the same page over and over again, and I wanted to ask "if he is reading a book, why can't he turn the pages?" In my mind, reading a book involved doing those two

things – otherwise you weren't reading a book, you were looking at the pictures. Isn't it odd, the things that stick in the mind?

There was also the sudden and unexpected death of mum's last surviving brother, my Uncle Arthur. Uncle Arthur had been driving to work when he began to feel unwell and so he parked his car on the side of the road. The motorist who was following behind, thinking that it was an unusual place for a car to be parked, stopped his own vehicle and went to see if everything was alright – he found Uncle Arthur dead behind the steering wheel. Uncle Arthur was only in his forties.

When I came home from school that day, I was surprised to find Dad there; I immediately panicked because this usually meant that Mum was unwell again. Mum suffered from a growing list of ailments, and both my sister and I never knew how mum would be when we returned from school. Sometimes she would be in the kitchen – the kettle on the hob, ready to make us a drink, on other occasions, she would be in bed – in a darkened room – suffering from the effects of a migraine. We just never knew what to expect.

On this particular day, I went into the kitchen and found dad waiting. He said, "Uncle Arthur has died". I thought he was talking about another uncle of the same name, an elderly man who was the brother in law of Grandma and so I asked "Is Grandma coming to stay?"

I remember how Dad looked at me with a totally puzzled and exasperated expression on his face. He repeated the phrase and looked towards the closed door which led to the living room, it was then I realised who he was talking about - mums' brother.

I remember asking dad if I should go in to see mum – he said "yes".

As quietly as I could, I slid the glass door along its runner and stepped into the room.

The thing that I remember most was the sight of my mum, just sitting – staring.
She didn't acknowledge the fact that I was home, not by a look or a word.
As I write this now I am feeling those feelings of shock and fear that I felt then.
Not knowing whether I should go out of the room or stay.
Say something- but I have no words – not even "sorry".
I just stood there, until Dad came and "rescued" me.

I recognise now, that she was totally locked into her grief, but then – I was just plain scared.

I remember wondering to myself if mum was sad that she couldn't be with her mum and dad and two brothers and I felt sad for her.

I know she believed that her family were watching us, and she would say to me, when I mentioned another occasion when I had smelt some aroma "That's your Granddad watching you".

There were also the deaths of dogs.

As I mentioned earlier, our two dogs at that time were called Lassie and Moss.

Lassie was a black and tan mongrel dog and she was definitely my Mums dog. Lassie used to carry a little rubber squeaky doll around with her and I very quickly learnt, that touching that doll invited Lassies' wrath in the form of snapping teeth. Only Mum, it seemed, was allowed to touch it.

Another memory of Lassie that I have is hearing her screams and howls if anyone invaded her space on the settee.

She would sit curled up next to Mum on the settee very contentedly, but woe betide the unsuspecting. If you chose to sit too close to her yourself; she would create such a sudden, ear splitting, scream and yelp, that anyone hearing it would have thought that she was in mortal peril and chastising her could result in a growl or a snap.

Moss on the other hand, was a gentle giant.

Mum and Dad had "rescued" him from a dog's home.

He was a large dog of mixed origin – a cross between a German Shepherd and some other large breed and was also black and tan, in colour.

Moss had had to move to the new house in the back of the removal van as Dad's black Ford car wasn't big enough for all of us, and having watched the doors of the van being shut against him (he was the last to be loaded) – it was with much relief that I watched him emerge at the other end, to see for the first time, his new, big garden.

One of Moss's pleasures was to be vacuumed. Our hoover was one of those cylindrical ones, with a long hose attached and every time Mum got the hoover out, Moss would sidle up to her, pushing against her legs, "insisting" that the nozzle was put on him. He would stand for ages delighting in the sensation of his hair and skin being sucked in ripples along his body.

The added bonus for Mum, was that his excess hair went directly into the hoover, and not on the floor, to be sucked up later.

Moss and I roamed freely around the garden and also liked to wander down the drive to the road – always keeping to the pavement – where he would have a "sniff" to see who had recently walked along it's way, then we would return to the garden and search between the bushes.

Our "secret" thing that we did together was to creep upstairs into Mum and dad' bedroom, where we would climb onto the blanket chest which was in front of the window. I would then open the window whereupon, both of us would climb out onto the flat roof of the bay window below, and survey any activity in the surrounding area, from our lofty position.

One day, to my horror, Moss jumped down onto the ground below, landing on all fours, onto the gravel and it was only as he sidled off, luckily uninjured, that my heart rate began to slow down.

As I raced downstairs to join him I made the decision that we would never climb out of that window again.

One morning as I was upstairs getting ready for school, I heard the voice of our neighbour, Mrs Trelfa, talking to Dad downstairs, in the hall.

Being nosy, and surprised by her visit so early in the morning, I began to descend the stairs.

"Stay up there", my dad shouted, as he rushed out of the house.

I sat on the stair and waited. I could hear Mum moving about downstairs and then I heard a drumming noise which sounded like the empty wheelbarrow being pushed along the gravel outside. Bemused, I rushed into Mum and Dads' bedroom and climbed onto the blanket chest to look out of the window. I remember being happy about this "thing" whatever it was, because the diversion meant that with luck, the school bus would go without this 8yr old on it.

Then I saw the white of my Dad's shirt through the hedge as he came up the drive.

The vision of my Dad pulling that wheelbarrow, which was failing to contain all of the lifeless body of Moss stopped my world from spinning.

I watched through my tears in horror, as Dad pulled that wheelbarrow down to the bottom of the garden, where, I noticed, the spade, was leaning up against the big apple tree.

I don't know how long it was before I descended the stairs and went out into the garden but as I approached, step by hesitating step, I heard dad say to Mum, "There's not a mark on him".
I was yet to find out what was wrong with Moss, but I knew he was just asleep, everyone was behaving as though he was dead and if they left him alone, then he would wake up. Dad mustn't bury him – Moss was just asleep.

Noticing me standing some distance away, Dad turned to mum and said "Send her to school – she'll be better at school".
I was beside myself in shock grief and fear and began to cry louder and louder.
Understanding my grief, Mum took me in the house - the school bus went without me.

Mum explained that Mrs Trelfa had seen Moss standing on the pavement, looking out across the road.
A van had been driven along the road and the driver had deliberately swerved into the kerb and part of the van had struck Moss on the head, killing him instantly.
The van hadn't stopped.

How I wished I could see that man and call him a murderer.

He had killed a beautiful, gentle, wonderful dog.

He had deliberately, taken my protector and my friend away from me.

Why?

Sometime after Moss's death, Lassie had a litter of puppies, diminishing her total – but not entire - infatuation with the rubber doll.

I had never known the delights and heartbreaks of caring and re-homing a puppy before now, but this litter, of which we kept one bitch who we called Meg – led to two further litters from Meg, from which, we kept one more bitch, (Mum and Dad had found a home for this puppy, but then the people said they didn't want her, and, unable to find another home, and as she was now answering to her name of Pup – we kept her). Megs' last litter resulted in us keeping a dog, who we named Shep. (More of Shep in Ch8)

These litter of puppies, all had the same father. He was a very handsome black mongrel dog called Timmy. Timmy lived down the road, and I loved to make a fuss of him when he visited us.

Shep was my favourite. He looked very like his Dad, only smaller, but it was to my great disappointment, that, as Shep became an adult, he barred Timmy from visiting us any more.

Shep would stand by the drive gate and growl as Timmy approached.

The tension between them built to a great crescendo one summer's day, resulting into a horrific dogfight, the first that I had ever seen.

17

I stood aghast amid the noise and dust, as Dad tried to intervene.

Discovering that their collars had become entwined, Dad rushed indoors, returning with a bucket of cold water, which he threw, with considerable force, over the two dogs.
Silence immediately fell, and both dogs shook themselves and walked off in opposite directions with only their dignity wounded.

Until I was 11 yrs old, my sister and I attended a private "day and boarding school". We went daily, as did the majority of the pupils, and our classmates, came from all over Cheshire and beyond.

Attending a school outside of my village and its' immediate area, meant that I had no contact with the other children in the village. During term time, myself and two of my friends, would occasionally spend weekends at each others' houses – on a sort of rota basis – but during the 8 week long summer holidays, we individually, had to amuse ourselves.

During the summer holidays, one of my favourite things to do was to hide in my "den" which was located between an old yew tree and the hedge. This hedge bordered a driveway which led to the house next door, and it was here that I would pretend to be an Indian Squaw.
Now, following an incident that I had had with the boy next door (told later on in this chapter) – I had pestered Dad to buy me a knife and was now the proud owner of my very own penknife.
With my knife, I would whittle sticks – then coat the pointed ends of them with red tile polish, (to simulate

heat) and build a fire whilst waiting for my Indian brave husband, to return home from his hunting trip.

The location of my den had the added bonus of providing a hiding place; from which I spied on anyone – or anything, that went past, and it was here that I practised the skill that I knew the Indians had – that of total silence whilst hiding amongst the undergrowth.

Being an outgoing, talkative child, (hopefully, not a nuisance or embarrassment – but there were times, when I must have been) I had no hesitation in latching myself onto various, very patient, adults – in my search of "something to do".

One such adult, who gave me "something to do" one summer, was Mr Carter.

Mr Carter worked selling fruit and vegetables, from his horse drawn cart.

His depot was located in our street and after some pestering from me (I would be about 9yrs old); he said that I could join him on his village round, one Friday morning. I was thrilled to bits, I loved horses, I loved the smell of this horse, I loved the smell of his leather harness, I loved the noise the horse made as he plodded his familiar route, I didn't like fruit very much – but never mind.

My "job" was to walk alongside the cart "On The Pavement" then, as we stopped at the customers house, (which in those days (1961ish), was practically every house) – I would go up the pathway, knock on the door, "Say Good Morning – Politely" and return to the waiting cart, clutching an empty shopping bag, a hand scribbled order, the money to pay for it, and, very often, a crust of stale bread for the horse.

Some people didn't bother to write their orders down, buying the same items every week. And these people would say to me; "I'll just have: -

5lbs of potatoes – no small ones, and NO very big ones.
2lbs of medium size carrots.
1 medium size cabbage
2 small onions
1/2lb of tomatoes
1 lettuce
4 apples
2 oranges – no make that 4 – the grandchildren are coming.
3 bananas
And half a dozen eggs – the brown ones – they taste nicer boiled".

Hoping that I had remembered everything correctly, I would then return to their door with the now, full to overflowing shopping bag, (being careful not to drop the eggs), which, unless the customer had given me an empty egg box to use, were in a brown paper bag and nestling in between 4 oranges. And of course, their change.

After the mornings work, we returned to the depot. The horse was fed and watered and then led down the street, past our house, to be turned out into a field, for his well-earned rest.
On the walk back to my house I would turn to Mr Carter and ask if I could go again the next Friday;
"If you're there by 8.30 sharp – then you can come" he would reply.

Mr and Mrs Jones moved into the general grocery shop at the end of our road and I quickly saw another opportunity for "something to do".

I would now be about 10 or 11yrs old and Mr and Mrs Jones agreed to find a job for me.
I was given this particular job, on the understanding that I would stay in the stock room at the back of the shop, and not get in the way of the ladies who worked part time, in the shop.

These were the days when purchases of loose items were placed into paper bags, which came in bundles. The bundles were held together at one corner with a piece of string, from which, the bags were then hung on a convenient nail under the counter. My job was to apply a rubber stamp, which imprinted the name and address of the shop, onto the white paper bags.
I took this job very seriously – inking the stamp carefully to avoid revealing only half of the address (wastage was frowned upon). Getting the stamp parallel to the bag, before pressing down hard (but not too hard). And most important of all, placing the stamp in the right place. In this case, the right place, I was instructed, was - slightly off centre and to the bottom right hand of the bag. This enabled the purchaser – on receipt of their filled bag – to still be able to read the address. Simple!

Other than my ultimate ambition to serve a customer in the shop (an ambition, I quickly realised, would never be fulfilled,) I set my sights on shelf filling, and it was a very grateful me, who, one happy day, prepared myself to replenish the shop shelves.
Standing in front of those shelves, (with their diminished stock of tinned peas, baked beans and

peaches), new stock at my feet, and armed with a large, black, felt tip pen – I set to work.

Every individual tin had its price written in felt tip pen, on the lid, and I felt very grown up as I checked the prices from a list I had been given, and marked the tins. However, I soon realised that this was actually quite a boring job to do and I became tired of concentrating in order to keep my handwriting "neat". More than that, the customers got in the way. I had been instructed that every time a customer came into the shop, I had to move the new tins out of the way, (so that they didn't trip on them), and return to the stockroom.
My "career" in the shop was short lived – but enjoyable.

There are other memories of the varied shops and their owners that stay with me; the shoe shop and its enticing smell of new leather.
The shoe shop, to which I was entrusted to go – by myself – at the age of 11yrs, in order to buy a new pair of school shoes. How grown up did I feel? Armed with the school regulations (black or brown in colour AND no more than an inch heel in height) running through my brain, and the money Mum had given me – I walked to the shop.
On hearing the doorbell ring, the man who owned the shop, came to serve me. He seemed surprised to see me standing there;
"Hello Lynn – are you on your own – what can I do for you?"
Having explained my needs, he began to bring out a selection of shoes for me to try on. I immediately fell in love with a black and brown pair which had eyelets, round which you twisted the laces. To my delight, the

heel (he measured it for me) was exactly one inch in height.

Just as I was making the decision to buy these shoes, his wife came into the shop and admired the shoes.

"I think they will be very good for school" she said.

He placed the shoes in their box and I handed the money over to him.

Mum seemed pleased with my choice, although she did question the durability of the eyelets!

It was some months later, that I learnt that Mum had called in to see the shop owner, prior to my visit – explaining what type of shoe I needed and roughly how much she wanted to pay, adding that she would be sending me on my own.

The whole scenario had been set up – but that didn't in any way, diminish the gratitude that I felt at being treated like an adult.

The hardware shop, where we bought our firelighters and paraffin, not forgetting the box of fireworks which Dad bought every year, just in time for Guy Fawkes Night. The same shop, to which I was sent one Friday morning on an errand from home.

Mum had a lady who came to clean the house and I used to "help" her, like I loved to "help" others.

One Friday morning she said to me, in my Mums presence; "You need elbow grease to scrub this floor – I've run out, would you go down to the hardware shop and ask them for a tin of it?"

Mum gave me some money, and off I went. "She must have run out of that smelly soft soap she usually used", I thought.

"Could I have a tin of elbow grease please?" I asked the owner.

He called into the rear of the shop to his son: "There's a young lady here who wants a tin of elbow grease – have we got any?"

His son emerged from the rear of the shop and the two of them stood and grinned at me.

He asked who had sent me and when I told him, he laughed and said, "She's pulling your leg – she means it's hard work scrubbing the floor – go home and tell her that we've run out"

I remember walking home, feeling very embarrassed and silly and a little bit cross.

And lastly, there was the smaller general grocers' shop, which had a bell fastened on the inside wall, above the door. The bell was a proper bell with a clanger and it was attached to the wall via a flat bendy piece of metal. Each time the door was opened, the bell went, "ding a ling a ling a ling a ling a ling".

The adults, whom I remember from that time in my life, were, with the odd exception – all very kind and caring. The village was one of those villages where everyone knew everyone else.

This was not an advantageous thing, I discovered, when, during my early teenage years – and hanging around the chip shop was the only entertainment on a winters night – there would always be someone to say to Mum the next day;

"I saw your Lynn last night – a gang of them there were on those seats near the chip shop – she must have been frozen to death in that short skirt!"

Next door to us, lived a family who had two boys.

The youngest was about the same age as me, the elder of the two, was about three years older – his name was David.

One summers evening, with my parents out at a meeting and my sister in the house "baby sitting" me, I wandered out into the garden. David, who would have been around 13yrs old at this time, appeared, wearing his scout uniform and a smug grin.

"I've got a knife," he boasted as he revealed his brand new sheath knife.

"Oh let me have a look," I asked, holding out my hand.

"You're too young to hold a knife – but I'll show you what I can do with it – I've been practising".

With that, he instructed me to stand about 4 feet away from the fence, with my feet slightly apart.
As the fence was a ridged mesh one and he could see through it, he studied the position of my feet and said, "Just move your feet a bit further apart".

"What are we going to do?" I asked, somewhat perplexed.

"I'm going to throw the knife as close to your feet as I can get it – stand still".

With that he held the knife aloft, holding onto the blade, and flung it over the top of the fence, towards my feet.

The blade cut into the grass, not far from my left foot.

"Oh" he exclaimed "I can get it nearer than that – pass it back to me".

"But it's my go now" I complained "I'll do it to you".

"No, I've said, you're too young – pass it me back"

And so the game continued – him throwing – me passing back.

At some point, my sister must have seen us from the window, and she hammered on the glass, shouting, "Stop That!"

The next thing I knew, I was being grabbed by the arm and being told how stupid I was, and to "Get in the house".
 "But David says it's alright – he's been practising" was my protest as I was bustled inside.

It was pointed out to me by my sister, how dangerous the game had been, she also pointed out all the ghastly things that could have happened, had that knife plunged onto my vital organs.
She was right, of course, and so were Mum and Dad, who, after being told of the episode by my sister – repeated, practically word for word, what she had said.

The game, I discovered, has a name, which is – "split the kipper". And my advice to anyone is: -

DO NOT TRY THIS AT HOME!

CHAPTER TWO

MUSIC AND ME

I grew up hearing a wide variety of different music. There was the organ music in the Chapel, piano music from Charlie Kunz, Mrs Mills and Russ Conway on the wireless, Dad's Rossini record, (the William Tell Overture being a favourite of both of us) and his much loved, gypsy violin record; Dad had learnt to play the violin as a boy (an instrument that when I hear it being played, is akin to chalk being scrapped down a blackboard) and whenever this record was played – it was time for me to disappear.

Choral music was also very also familiar to me, as both Mum and Dad, although no longer members, had sung in the Nothwich Festival Choir and every December – as soon as I could be relied upon to "sit still and be quiet", I was taken along with my sister to hear the annual performance of Handle's Messiah.

I quickly learned to love going to these recitals, the power of the voices, the harmonies, the sopranos - high above the tenors, all these things made the hair at the back of my neck stand on end, and as I learned to read music, the joy of sharing mum's copy of "The Messiah", which both Mum and Dad always took with them, gave me the feeling that I was part of the choir, singing the high notes along with the sopranos.

London Road Methodist Church, Northwich, was "our church" and it was there that I attended three times every Sunday. I have many happy memories of that wonderful building, the people I met and grew up with, the Sunday School Anniversaries and subsequent "Outings" to Southport or New Brighton but the one outstanding experience was Miss Wilkinson and the pipe organ.

Congregation numbers had begun to fall and with it Sunday School attendance, on occasions I would be the only one of my Sunday School class to turn up and it was on these occasions that I was permitted to sit next to Miss Wilkinson as she "ran through" the hymns for that evening and selected other pieces to play on that mighty pipe organ.

So there I would sit, the vibration of the music all around me, the thump of the "stops" as they were pulled in and out, the ease with which Miss Wilkinson's hands and feet moved over the manual's and foot pedals, the musical chords which filtered right into your body. Brilliant!

I have never experienced anything quite like this since then and I am grateful to have been given the opportunity to experience it once in my life – time. Miss Wilkinson "you were brilliant, thank-you".

Mum and Dad kept all the Bibles' and Hymn Books that had belonged to past family members displayed on the top shelf of the family bookcase. The majority of the Hymn books were" tune" books and I had handled them many times, wishing and expecting, that one day I would have my very own "tune" book.

To commemorate - what was to us - the remaining congregation - the sad closure of the Sunday School and ultimately the closure and subsequent demolition of London Road Methodist Church. I was presented with my very own Methodist Hymnal (with tunes), the inscription inside noting the date – 9th October 1966.

Another one to add to the collection; my book now sits with the others, on the same shelf, in the same bookcase, in my living room.

The organ, I am pleased to say, was dismantled and re-assembled into a Church in Wales.

Also in that bookcase is a small bible, which belonged to a man, I had never met, but whose daughter, (12years or so older than me) I was friends with.
Susan was a neighbour and between the ages of 8 and 12, she was my friend, whether she liked it or not!
Susan lived with her mother when I first knew her and it was after the death of her mother that I be-friended her. There must have been many many times when she didn't want my company, but she never turned me away. I used to go to see her in the evenings when she returned from work, on the understanding that I didn't go before 7.30pm. I can remember now, straining at the leash, waiting for a television programme to finish, marking the allotted time, my mother watching, ready to pounce if I moved too soon.

Susan introduced me to coffee with a large dose of condensed milk; not in a cup, but in a glass with a colourful plastic holder (I thought this was very "grown – up") – pineapple upside down cake (a speciality of hers) and opera.
We would sit and listen in silence to her records and of course as the operas were mostly in Italian I had absolutely no idea what "they" were singing about, but it seemed to me that opera was very sad.
Susan would occasionally relate part of the story, but more often than not she would disappear into a world where she appeared to be completely alone with only the music for company, her eyes would close and there would be no movement from her; at these times I would sit as still as possible, staring at her – wondering where she had gone - and trying not to breath too loudly

knowing that if I disturbed the moment, I would no longer be welcome.
Susan showed me what a person looked like when they were totally engrossed in music.

When I was around 12yrs old Susan moved away and it was while she was sorting her things, ready for the move, that she gave me the Bible that had once belonged to her Dad, along with a framed watercolour painting he had done. I don't know her reasons for giving these things to me, none were given at the time as I recall, but I was, and still am, grateful for these momentoes and the memories and fondly keep them all.

I recognise now, that all through my life, profound and poignant happenings and meetings have usually been marked with the receiving of an object, a keep-sake, the energy of the happening or meeting being held within it, in the same way as a precious crystal holds within it's form, energy, knowledge and it's own unique healing power.
Tapping into these forces (psychometry) will be mentioned at a later stage in my story.

Remembering these people, these moments and occasions, makes me understand how fortunate I have been in my life. There have been so many people who have allowed me to share in their lives, taught me a lesson on which I would draw in future times, so many happy experiences and memories, so much guidance.

I began piano lessons probably when I was around nine or ten years old, with the same music teacher in school, who was teaching my sister to play.

Miss Whetherby was a mild, lovely lady, but when it came to the importance of "practice", she was very strict; "practice makes perfect Lynn", she would say.
Posture was also very important, to Miss Whetherby.
A straight back and hands were imperative and an aid that she insisted on using to achieve this - was the thrupenny bit. To those of you that are unfamiliar with this coin, the thrupenny bit was a twelve-sided coin, valued at three old pennies. One coin was placed on the back of each of my hands and I had to play, without them falling off.

I can remember sitting at the piano – back straight – a coin on each hand - stumbling through a piece of music as she slapped the top of the piano with her open hand, beating out the tempo that I should have been keeping time to. Her other form of "torture" was the metronome; how I hated that thing (I own one myself – but it still frightens me). Miss Whetherby taught me the basics of reading music and with her encouragement I did pass one rudimentary exam. I knew I didn't have the dedication, my wish was to play - not to learn to play.

My sister did have dedication and the willingness to learn, and she passed several exams and now retains far more knowledge on the subject than I ever bothered to learn.

By this time, I was about to leave this school to enter the world of Secondary Modern, and the scales, the practice and that dreaded metronome would be left behind – at least for a short time.

As so often happens in life, just as my friend Susan and her opera moved away, I met Miss Jones.

Miss Jones was the music teacher at my Secondary Modern school.

At that time "music" was a lesson on the timetable, along with English and Maths etc: and it was during those first few weeks of term that she announced that auditions would be taking place for the school choir. When I say auditions, it was more of a case of if you were keen and could "hold a tune" you were in.
I was in!
Being admitted into the school choir gave me and my friend Lizzy the confidence to join a chapel choir,
Lizzy and I were part of the amalgamated "Northwich and surrounding district" choirs when the Sunday evening television programme "Songs of Praise" came to Northwich Parish Church to record an edition.
Lizzy and I sang soprano, we went to all the rehearsals, we were ready and eager to be on the television.
It was very exciting!
However; as the amalgamated choirs came together, it was obvious that there were too many sopranos (where had they all come from?) Lack of young sopranos within our own chapel choir had been the reason Lizzy and I had been invited to join in the first place!
We were asked to sing alto instead.
This was a bitter blow to me, my chance of singing soprano with a large choir, just like in all those recitals I had sat through – gone.
Looking on the bright side, there was still the "probability" of appearing on television. Wrong again.
We were both placed behind a large church pillar, and what's more!! – we discovered, during the television screening - "They" didn't even show the offending pillar!

Being a member of Miss Jones's school choir was a much more relaxed affair. We would perform occasional concerts within the school, performing renditions from musicals such as South Pacific, West

Side Story and of course The Sound of Music. Another bonus for a choir member was that we were sometimes excused from other lessons for extra rehearsal time, as a concert date approached.

I have always remembered the advice given to us all by Miss Jones before a concert took place, it went something like; Enjoy yourselves, sing out – so that you can be heard at the back of the room and smile, to which she added – choose a member of the audience and keep smiling at them; the theory being, that if we looked as though we were enjoying ourselves, then that member of the audience would enjoy themselves and probably clap louder and longer.

Sensible advice for anyone who has to stand up in public and "perform".

Listening to music was also part of our lessons, particularly classical music.

Growing up listening to choral music taught me to hear and focus on the pitch of a soprano above a tenor, to learn a basic melody. The years of singing hymns in chapel, alongside tenors like my Dad, gave me a love of harmony, but being asked and trying to - pick out the notes and repeating them -as they had been played by a flautist, in the midst of a complete orchestra wasn't quite as easy.

Learning to focus on that one instrument amongst other much louder instruments was such an important lesson for me.

Listening took on a whole new meaning for me.

Listening to music in this way has the added benefit of revealing more of the energy of the piece and it's sublets of composition allowing "characters" essential to its story to emerge.

I resumed my relationship with scales and the dreaded metronome when Miss Jones agreed to give me piano lessons out of school hours. She produced some lovely music for me to learn, but I fell into the bad habit of only practising those pieces or even just parts of those pieces that I enjoyed the most.

It was obvious to Miss Jones what I was doing and she pointed out it to me that it appeared to be only those pieces of music that had a "flat" in them that I enjoyed. I knew this to be true. When presented with a new piece, I would look to see if it contained "sharps" or "flats" if it were the former I would inwardly groan, if it were the later – well I would try.

It wasn't a fact that "flats" were any easier to play than a "sharp", I just liked the sound more.

It was obvious that in regard of playing the piano, I had no true commitment.

I had always known that my reason for wanting to play in the first place was simple, I wanted to play like Armon did, I wanted Armon to play through me.

Yes, the idea of making music myself appealed to me, but without commitment and hard work I was never going to progress.

So it was that I abandoned the piano lessons - much to the relief of Miss Jones I would think- not to mention my parent's pocket.

I still occasionally play now on my electronic keyboard, which, at the press of a button, contains every instrument you would care to mention. Technology can be a wonderful thing!

My teenage years were spent listening to the music of the day and going to local dances with girls from school. There we would be, in a group, dancing round our handbags – a popular Friday and Saturday night activity.

Sunday night, I, like many other of my peers, would be listening to the "Top Twenty" hits as broadcast by Radio Luxembourg and received through my little "Dansette" transistor. Because this broadcast went on till midnight and long after Dad had shouted up the stairs "have you turned you light out yet?" to which I always replied "Ye-ees", I had to listen under the bedclothes, "tuning in" with the aid of a torch.

OK it was a little lie! This is probably when I learnt to be a "night" person as opposed to a "morning" person.

At this point in the story you will probably be waiting for me to tell you the name of the first record I owned - many people can recall this important event. You will no doubt be expecting to read that I have kept it all this time and you would be right, unfortunately - I CAN'T FIND IT!!

I do know that it's a 45rpm by McGuiness Flint but the title eludes me. Sorry about that!

There is one more person that I must mention in this chapter and that is Mr Trelfa. Like Susan, he was also a neighbour.

Mr and Mrs Trelfa had a growing family of their own and so were always busy, and yet Mr Trelfa still found time for me. Mr Trelfa had a metalwork shop at home and to an eight or nine-year-old child as I was, all the machinery, the curly metal filings and the tools hanging up, were a fascination. I remember being invited to stand just inside the room and being warned; "do not touch anything – do not pick up any of the metal filings, they are Very sharp, do not move your feet, the metal on the floor could go through your shoes".

I would root myself to the spot - these stern warnings, somehow adding to the mystery and wonder of spending time with Mr Trelfa.

Mr Trelfa played the trombone in a local Silver Band and very occasionally I witnessed him play it as he practised.
Such a strange looking instrument, I thought, and I could only imagine - in my child like way - that it must take a lot of blowing to make the sound come out of its' curling folds.
Not only did he introduce me to the trombone, but one day he asked me if I would like to listen to a record. Memory tells me that the record was an old 78rpm. What I am sure of, is that this was the first time I heard the "Trumpet Voluntary".
I loved the sound of that trumpet and they way the notes went up and down so quickly. I still wonder now, how it is that so many musical notes can emanate from that one instrument.

NB For those of you who may be tempted to listen to this piece of music for your self, I have now discovered that it is apparently, wrongly accredited to Henry Purcell, when in fact it was written by Jeremiah Clarke…. and there's another funny thing, Clarke was Susan's surname. Doesn't the Universe work in a wonderful way!

I have always remembered Mr and Mrs Trelfa fondly – it was Mrs Trelfa who took me, along with her children, on my first picnic. Over the years, (with the exception of one occasion, of which more later) our only contact was the annual Christmas card and so it was a shock to answer the phone one day to find Mrs Trelfa on the other end of the line, telling me that, sadly - Mr Trelfa had died.

In response to the news, I told her how much I treasured the memories of which I have just written and her response was, "well I've got some photographs of the work shop – I'll send you one".
It duly arrived and has been added to my collection of photographic memories.

By the age of 16yrs, I had left the chapel and the choir behind, gone through Secondary School, and surprised Mum and Dad by the announcement that I wanted to go to Sixth Form College – my average GCSE and GCE results, earning me a place there.
It was at the Sixth Form College that I met my husband John (he noticed me on the first day of term, I waited until day two), when, as we passed in the corridor, I said to myself – "I have just seen the man I am going to marry".

I will always remember my "Religious Studies" teacher Mr Shambrook. It was he who said to me on the evening of Prize Giving after I had recently learnt that I had failed my two "O – levels" - "You may have failed your "O – levels", but at least you have found John".
In that one moment I felt that Mr Shambrook knew everything about me.

Oh, and the reason I was at the Prize Giving, Mr Shambrook had put forward my name to receive a prize – "For Effort".
The only prize I had ever been awarded at school.

In March 1974 John and I were married, we walked down the aisle to the strains of J.S. Bach's Toccata & Fugue in D Minor, a piece we both loved.

In general our musical preferences were poles apart, John listening to the likes of Cream, Jethro Tull and BobDylan. Johns' Ravi Shankars' Sitar music brought back memories of my Dad's Gypsy music – time to disappear again! Likewise my eclectic mix of James Last and his Orchestra, The Bee Gees, Demis Rousos, Honky Tonk piano music (which John bought for me) were not exactly music to his ears either!

But then - we always had Queen.

Whichever genre of music I chose to play I would usually turn the record player up so that the music was loud
"Bouncing off the walls" sort of loud - enabling me to feel the vibration and energy of it.
Background music was of no interest to me and very often I found myself playing the same track repeatedly, which, on reflection, must have really irritated John, or anyone who had the misfortune to live nearby.
Of course many people can relate to the fact that a piece of lively music can help remove the tedium of housework, or the emulsioning of the living-room walls but when I was in my 20s and early 30s I really began to feel the need to work with music and experience it's affects on my body and my emotions.

I would shut myself in a bedroom where I had put a record and tape player and, with all my music within reach, and sitting cross-legged on the floor - I would begin.

These sessions always followed the same pattern and depending on my mood, they had different beginnings. The pattern was.:

To play a piece or pieces of music that portrayed my mood/emotion until I felt myself shifting into another emotion.
Then I would change the music to reflect that mood or emotion.

These sessions were a roller coaster of emotions, I would smile, cry, "dance" using my upper body in time to the music, cry again – I merely allowed myself to follow wherever the music took me.

I would repeat this pattern until I knew I had completed the circle of emotions as many times as I needed to - each session ending with me being in a happy, contented frame of mind, I knew that this was very important and the object of the exercise.

Sometimes the need to work in this way was my own – on other occasions I knew I was being told to go and do it - driven to do it, either way, I always benefited from these sessions feeling happier and more energetic afterwards.

It was during this time that I was guided to listen to a particular piece of music in order to heal the hurt I still felt, after the death of our much loved and missed, old English Sheepdog – Trampas.
(I will tell you more about Trampas – later in the book).

The singer – Nana Mouskouri – the title "Try To Remember".

One line in particular is – "Try to remember the kind of September, where no one wept except the Willow"

I cried bucketful's when I listened to this track - but gradually the words and music, together with the wonderful clarity of Nanas' voice, brought about a healing.
Happy memories; the joy of knowing Trampas and having him in our lives, plus the knowledge that he was well again and still playing - to a new audience now in spirit - overcame the pain of loss.
Although I have to admit that I have wiped away one or two tears as I have been remembering and writing about him now.

Our hurt reminds us that we loved.

Those sessions quickly became a very precious and important resource for me then, as they are now.
I could hear the sopranos, high above the tenors.
I would listen for the "Flute"
I began to hear notes that I hadn't heard before.
I could dance, whilst sitting on the floor.

CHAPTER THREE

SHE LOOKED BRILLIANT!

In order for me to share my story with you, it is necessary to relate relevant important times in my childhood and early adulthood. Notably these events surround death, because to a Medium, death is very relevant.

I am about to narrate my journey of progressive communication, and how death was a key for me to unlock my physic energy.

However, because three of the following deaths are my parents and my husband John's mum, and because John and I have a sister each, I will respectfully, only recount those moments that are pertinent to the progression of my story.

Those in Spirit, who are assisting me to write this book, will guide and help me – as they have just assisted in the writing of this piece.

In 1980 when I was 28yrs old, my paternal grandmother died.

Grandma has left me with some funny memories, mostly things she would say.

Every Tuesday, Grandma would take the two bus rides to our house, arriving in time for tea.

She would always be expected, and would always arrive at the same time of day. Knowing all this however, never prepared me for the sudden "unexpected" appearance of her smiling face, peering out of the darkness of a winters' night, through the kitchen window – accompanied by the sudden rap on the windowpane.

However much I tried to prepare myself – every Tuesday – I would jump out of my skin.

Even now, all these years later and when it's dark outside - I often stand, busying myself at the sink in front of the window and half expect that rap on the window pane.

On Christmas Eve she would come to stay for two days and being December it was invariably "Jackie Frost out there".

Usually there was a "Western" film on television with "Shooty Bangs" in it.

"Has this got Shooty Bangs in it?" she would ask.

"I don't like films with Shooty Bangs".

Although she didn't like "Shooty Bangs!" She was the only one in our family who did enjoy a circus - (Ugh!). Therefore on Boxing Day afternoon you would find us all watching the annual screening of Billy Smarts' circus on the television.

She also loved Tom Jones. She had been to a Tom Jones concert with the "over sixties" club and they had all been invited to meet him in person. Apparently on meeting with him, he had kissed the back of her hand, a gesture which had become a treasured memory. Needless to say, if Tom Jones featured in a variety programme – we all had to watch in a reverent silence.

Like most grandmothers she also used to talk during a television programme, spotting someone she recognised and asking, what their name was and what programme they had been in before. By the time one of us had remembered, we had all lost the plot!

It's a strange thing, but I have noticed as the years have gone by, that I am now "suffering" from the same phenomenon. Whilst watching a television programme, I hear myself asking John; "Oh is that thingy, who used to be in whatsits? What's' her name? You know who I mean – what's' her name?"

Grandma had lived alone since the death of granddad in 1954; she worked throughout her life and had a very sociable life (in fact she was rarely at home). Much of her social life involved the Methodist church. Illness never seemed to come her way, not even a cold, but occasionally, in the last eighteen months of her life, she had said she didn't want to be eighty. It seemed to us all, that another twenty years were probable.
Approximately two weeks after her eightieth birthday, she died of a stroke, after a short stay in hospital.

During the process of comparing Grandmas' death, with that of my Uncle Arthurs' - questions came to my mind.

"How is it possible for a man in his forties, with no signs of illness, to be here one day, and gone the next?"
"How is it possible for a lady of 79yrs, who had no major, or even minor ailments, say she didn't want to be eighty, and then die two weeks after her eightieth birthday?"

"What, if any, influence do we have over our own departure?"
"Is death pre – ordained, accidental, or purely inevitable?"

Having witnessed funerals from a distance as a child, in no way prepared me for going to one.

APRIL 1980.

Looking at bouquets and wreaths, after everyone had left, didn't prepare me for the coldness I felt as I watched her coffin being lowered into its' grave, nor was I prepared for that feeling of "non finality" that I felt, as I walked away from the grave – yet to be filled in.

And years of being around, and holding treasured books and objects, didn't prepare me for helping to clear out grandma's bungalow.

Handling her possessions was a very strange feeling, I felt guilty and nosy. I began by asking Mum; "Shall I open this drawer? – Shall I go in this cupboard?"

As time went on Mum and I (my sister was heavily pregnant at the time, and was stopped from helping} noticed that there wasn't as much to clear as we thought there would have been.

Grandma loved bedding and she used to buy lots of it and store it in a blanket chest – but the question was, "Where was it?" The chest only had a few items in it.

We came to the conclusion that she must have given it away.

I remember there were other things that we had expected to find, like the little Christmas tree that always stood on the sideboard every Christmas, it was nowhere to be found.

Had she thrown these things away? Had she known she wouldn't be there next Christmas?

There was definitely no way I was prepared for this process and seeing the things that couldn't be found a new home, placed into plastic bags to be thrown away - was sad.

One of the things that did find a good home was one of grandma's hats!

A neighbour knocked on the door soon after mum and I arrived – actually, it was before we had taken our coats off - and described one hat in particular;

"I wonder if I could have it as a keepsake? That is if no one else has asked for it", she added.

Mum found the hat and handed it to her;

"Thankyou" she said – I've always liked this hat" she explained – "I'll miss her" and with that she went off down the path.

Another object that found a good home was Granddads pendulum clock.

The clock had always been in the same place above the sideboard and when Granddad was alive, only he wound it up. Apparently the clock was made to chime on the quarter, half hour and hour but granddad had "Fixed it" and it only chimed on the half hour and hour.

I stood and watched as Dad walked over to the clock, he turned and said to me "would you like the clock?" I was surprised and thrilled to bits. I'd naturally assumed that dad would take the clock home with him - other than a watch and chain, it was the only thing I knew of, that had belonged to his dad - my Granddad.

I was absolutely thrilled and grateful and the very proud keeper of Granddads' clock.

JANUARY 1986.

Elsie: my mother-in-law had died the previous day:

As soon as my key touched the lock in the door, I knew Elsie was inside the house.

I paused and my stomach "flipped over".

What should I do? Should I turn and walk away? What did she want? Why was she doing this to me?

These feelings were very different to any I had had before when I had felt spirit around me – this was scary.

I took a deep breath and opened the door slowly, but I didn't step inside.
As usual, the two dogs – our Old English Sheepdog; Boodlewood Pensive Prince, or Trampas as we called him, and Osmart Black Panther - Muppet to us - a Bearded Collie – nearly knocked me over with their enthusiastic welcome. Ignoring their antics, I went into the living room and stood still; "I know you're here, What do you want?" "Why are you here?" I demanded

"*I'm on the stairs*", came the message in my head.

I went towards the door that led to the hallway, opened it, and went and stood at the bottom stair, and as I looked upwards to the top step all my initial feelings of fear and trepidation, mixed with false bravado – left me, and were replaced by peace, love and happiness.

Elsie stood, smiling at me. She looked brilliant.
She was wearing a green and white print frock and it was obvious to me that she had just had her hair done.
"Why are you here?" I asked.
"*I've just come to tell you that I'm alright*" was the answer.
"Oh good" I replied.
We stood smiling at one another – and then she disappeared.
To this day, I have never seen Spirit quite as vividly as when I saw Elsie for that first time.

Feeling happy that Elsie was already well and happy was great – but what would I say to John?

Still reeling from seeing her so vividly and of our face-to-face telepathic conversation – and mindful of John's grief - I decided to say nothing.

This decision played on my mind. I knew she was well, she looked well and happy, she had said she was. I felt as though I was the only person to know this, and I wasn't sharing the information with John.

Of course, knowing that Elsie was happy in no way stopped the pain of her loss – the wishing that you could just ring and tell her something - the sadness that she died too young, all the other emotions that are part of grief.

I continued with my silence, but it seemed that Elsie was going to force the issue.

Things began to disappear in the house; little things that I knew were "in the drawer" were not to be found, and then a few days or even weeks later these "things" would re–appear. Both John and I were "victims" of these phenomena.

I knew it was Elsie playing these games, they were gentle funny games. The strange thing is that I remember thinking "Why is she doing this?" it never entered my head to ask, "How is she doing this?" It was my belief and understanding that those in Spirit could do anything they wished, where-ever and when-ever they wished; freedom belonged to those in Spirit: only later in life did I realise that it is only the restriction that we physical beings put onto ourselves that prevent us from having that same freedom.

It must have been about the first time in my life so far when I was afraid to speak up, however, plucking up the courage one day, after John and I had both been looking for yet another "thing" that had gone missing

I said, "This is your mum's sense of humour, she's doing this".

To my relief, John said that he'd had the same thought, and we both laughed.

From that time on it became easier to talk about her – we knew that she was still near – watching what we were doing – and we knew that she was happy.

At times these games could be irritating, and one or both of us would call out, "OK – where have you put it?" the answer coming sometime later when the said item revealed itself once more.

Another instance when Elsie returned was during the summer of 1986, when our much-loved dog Trampas had become ill.

He had been off colour during the day and worsened during the evening. By 11 o'clock that night, Trampas was unable to stand. (We later found out that he had a virus). Having rung the vet, and whilst waiting for a home visit – I felt Elsie come into the room. Feeling upset and anxious and kneeling down on the floor with Trampas, I felt Elsie come and stand beside us. I immediately panicked, believing that Elsie had come to take Trampas with her.

"Go away – you can't have him – Go away" I silently shouted. She left.

Trampas recovered from that illness but on the morning of 5th November that year and after two weeks of him "not being himself" it was clear to John and I that he was very ill.

Again, whilst waiting for another home visit from the vet, I knelt down beside him. Elsie arrived but kept her distance. I laid my hand on Trampas's back and looked into his blue eyes, he gazed up at me and I heard him say to me "I've had enough". I recognised the "smell of death" that I had smelt before on the day our 12yr old black mongrel Shep had been put down, some 12 years earlier.

My heart sank.

The vet arrived and decided to take him to the surgery for tests.

Two hours later, while Trampas was still under anaesthetic undergoing tests, the vet rang to tell us that he had cancer of the spleen. John, the vet, and I decided that the best solution for Trampas was to put him to sleep immediately.

Boodlewood Pensive Prince died, 3 months before his 12th birthday.

Trampas's birthday had been the 14th of February 1976 – Valentines Day – and he had brought so much love, laughter and delight into our lives and now on the morning of the 5th November (Guy Fawkes night – a night of loud celebration in the UK) he had been put to sleep, (he never liked fireworks!)

Our last picture of him was him, standing stoically, in the rear of the vet's car as she drove away. The vet said that he had stood all the way on the journey - although given his condition – she didn't know how he had managed it.

Trampas had always taken everything in his stride; nothing had ever fazed him – not even his own impending death.

I implored Elsie to look after him and of course she did, bringing him back to visit on numerous occasions.

Trampas had been in our lives for over eleven and a half fantastic years. Every moment a memorable one, not the least being the day we met him.

John and I hadn't been looking to buy an Old English Sheepdog puppy, John was working at that time as a press photographer and had gone to photograph a "Champion of Champions" for a magazine, of course being "dog mad" it was too great an opportunity for me to miss so I tagged along.
Over a cup of tea, after the photographs had been taken, the breeder left the room for a few minutes and returned with this puppy who, although he was around five months old, was small for his age and scrawny – the runt of the litter – soon to be known as Trampas!
From the very first time John and I had met Trampas (he walked off with John's car keys, which had been put on a coffee table, as if to say "Come on – shall we go now") we loved him.

You've probably heard the phrase "Taken to heart" – you may have experienced it, well I had no understanding of what that really felt like until that morning of the 5th November 1986, when I felt the spirit of Trampas leaving my heart, like a piece of me being torn out – a feeling that I would feel several times in the future – at the departure of a Guide, as our combined energies were separated: it always hurts.

Up to this point in my life I had always talked and laughed while asleep but for around 3 months, after the death of Trampas this all stopped, it seemed that I was so angry and upset I had nothing to say to "them".

As I have been writing this story, and therefore re living it, I am struck by my rudeness and audacity towards Elsie, a lovely, lively person who was one of life's best "mothers in law" you could wish to meet. There was no way I would have spoken to her in such a fashion whilst alive and I believed I respected those in Spirit. I recognise now, how far I have come along this journey and how far I had to travel.

It would not be until 1994, when I would meet William – who I refer to as my "first working Guide"

that I would begin to understand what working as a medium entailed. How disciplined and respectful a good medium has to be. William was and still is VERY big on discipline and respect!

Whoever it was that had written the song "My Way" must have been inspired to write it after meeting William in a previous lifetime!

CHAPTER FOUR

THE DAY THOU GAVEST

To be honest with you I have found this chapter difficult to begin, having been given the title whilst writing chapter 2.

I felt as though I must tell you about all my mother's illnesses, which appeared (according to her) to begin when I was born.

To tell you how, at one stage in her life, because of her Rheumatoid Arthritis, she could no longer walk

and how, after three months in the Royal Devonshire Hospital in Buxton, Dad, John and I arrived to see her walking arm in arm with her doctor.

To tell you how "well" the steroids made her look and how her stubbornness kept her going.

But this story is about my journey of development and so, I "asked Spirit" for help in order to continue writing - the question being - "How does chapter 3 start?"

"I remember - because I remember too" was the reply from Mum.

OCTOBER 1990.

I remember standing at the bottom of the hospital bed and looking at mum as she lay there, very weak now, and as she looked at me she silently said,

"I'm dying now – but I will see you again"

I replied,

"I know – I'll see you again".

Then I just walked out of the room for the last time – leaving John, Dad and my sister to that terrible ordeal of taking it in turns – and waiting.

I walked because I couldn't find the courage to stay, and that clear and precise conversation kept running through my mind.

I was staggered to have been able to communicate with Mum in this way. "Had we done this before?" I didn't know, "If not – Why not?"

Yes, I thought, I had spoken to Elsie after her death – but that had not surprised me.

Yes, I often heard conversations in my head – only to have, or hear, those conversations repeated – days or weeks afterwards – I was used to that

My emotions were all over the place. I was fearful of Mum dying, in shock - knowing that this time she would not be coming out of hospital, after all, she had just told me so. I was also angry that I had not known that we could communicate in this way. I was happy, but sad. I felt that so much time had been wasted between us – dealing with day to day issues,

I remember asking all mums family in spirit to be waiting for her, she would be back with them all at last.

I also remember asking John, who had been there at the time of this conversation, if he had noticed anything "strange", he said he knew something special had happened, he had seen "the moment", he said "I know I've witnessed something". And through tears and gulps, I told him what had been said.

Mum died at approximately 4pm on 28th October 1990.

John told me how, the previous night, Mum had reminded him to "turn the clocks back" as British Summer Time had come to an end.

Mum had repeatedly reminded us of this event over the previous years, beginning about two weeks in advance, and it had become a bit of a joke between us all.

Now, when I "turn the clocks back" I very often say to her, "I'm turning the clocks back – OK."

The following days were spent attending to all the formalities of arranging the funeral, informing relatives and friends, and watching and caring for Dad, who, following the removal of a lung as the result of cancer, wasn't in good health himself.

As the funeral neared, I became increasingly apprehensive about singing one of the hymns we had chosen – The Day Thou Gavest – to me the singing of this hymn would be the acknowledgement that I would be saying goodbye. It had been a favourite hymn of Mum's yet her voice would often falter when she was singing it.

The day before the funeral I found out that both Dad and my sister had the same dread.

It has become one of those hymns, which bring tears to my eyes every time I hear it and if I sing it - my voice falters.

At the beginning of December my sister handed me an advent calendar that mum had bought for me. (Both my sister and I received one every year). And along with that; there was also a set of three wooden spoons, which had ducks on the handles. Mum had obviously begun her preparations for Christmas early and at some point, had told my sister where to find these items.

I hung the calendar on the wall, knowing that this was going to be another difficult Christmas, as it had been, just before Elsie had died.

When Dad was told that he had lung cancer and would have to have a lung removed he said with conviction "It will be alright – it isn't my time yet" and indeed he appeared to recover well, however, following the death of my mother his health began to deteriorate and in late May 1991 he was back in hospital.

Ward 2, Leighton Hospital was a ward well known to me and my family and to John's family, we knew the staff and they grew to know us over the years, and it was during an evening visit that Dad asked me to find a new home for his dog Nell.
Nell had been put into a local kennels for the duration of his stay as neither my sister nor I, who both had dogs of our own, could not take her in. Dad wouldn't be talked out of his decision to have her re-homed and it was with reluctance that we asked the owner of the kennels, if she could help, bearing in mind that Nell was already a rescue dog and also middle aged.

It was also after visiting Dad one evening that the ward Sister asked John and I to go to her office.
She had arranged for Dad to go into a hospice:

JUNE 1991.

I was very nervous as I walked hand in hand with John towards the Hospice doors, unlike John, I had never been inside one before.

What a peaceful brightly decorated place it was, the staff were wonderful, and when we were shown into the four bedded bay where Dad was, it was obvious that he was happy, comfortable and relaxed – he even "cracked" a few jokes and was looking forward to cheese on toast for his tea.

We had been told that Dad would stay there for a couple of weeks and during that two weeks, as his medication was reviewed and altered he became happy and comfortable

One of the images that burnt onto my mind, was walking into the bay on a Saturday and seeing three beds occupied by three elderly men, (my Dad being one of them) who were all fast asleep and snoring, whilst in the corner of the room, the television was showing the Trouping of the Colour.

All three of these men had probably served in the Armed Forces during the war, they had survived that, and now here they were, nearing life's end, whilst other soldiers pledged their allegiance to Queen and Country. It seemed ironic to me, and the sight of those three men sleeping, whilst the brass band was playing on the television was, for me, a sad and haunting experience.

I remember the afternoon I went to see Dad; the afternoon I stood at the bottom of his bed whilst he was sleeping, and I saw that he was dying – saw that he wasn't really inside his body anymore, saw that he was disappearing.

I went home, (a journey of about ten minutes) not having spoken to him and as I sat in my chair looking through the window and through my tears, I noticed that a hole had appeared in the sky, a bright sunshiny hole, and it seemed to be hovering over the position of the Hospice.

"Go to the Light – Go up into the Light Dad" I repeated.

We got the call to go to the Hospice in the early hours of the morning and even though we were only a short distance away, John and I didn't make it in time, neither did my sister who had further to travel.

One of the nursing staff had stayed with him, for which we were very grateful, and Dad, well he just looked as though he was asleep.

Talking to my sister the next day she said that as she was leaving from the previous evening visit, Dad had said goodbye to her and then said, "Say goodbye to Lynn".

It seems as though Dad had known that "now was his time".

The next day, I returned to Ward 2 Leighton Hospital to let them know that Dad had died and to thank them for their kindness, care and arranging for Dad to go into the Hospice. Sister wasn't on duty but the Staff Nurse who we had known for such a long time was. She surprised me by saying that she had already been told by the Hospice of the news – I can only assume that they had asked to kept informed. She asked me to let her know when the funeral was, which I did.

On the day of the funeral and as we were walking out of the Chapel behind the coffin – there she was. I was so touched by the effort she must have made to be there.

I only had a moment to grab her hand and to say thankyou; her presence meant so much to me.

The following Christmas John and I were surprised to receive a Christmas card from "All on Ward 2", and for the following 3years - cards were always exchanged at this time of year.

It was also obvious that "they" were looking after Nell because the day after Dad died, the owner of the kennels rang to say that she had found a new home for her, with a family in the same area where Mum and Dad had lived. The owner of the kennels suggested that we met the people in order to assure ourselves that Nell would be going to a good home and so my sister went along and returned from the visit very happy.
I will always be grateful to that family for taking Nell into their home - it was something to be happy about.

My mother's parents had died 15 months apart and now my Mum and Dad had died within nine months of each other. I felt like "orphan Annie".
As well as getting on with our own lives, my sister and brother in law and John and I, had shared the responsibility of caring for Mum and Dad over the later years.
Now, there would be no more cleaning, cooking, running around and - being on call.
No more following the Ambulance with it's blue flashing lights, lighting up the dark road ahead.
No more urgent, or not so urgent, telephone calls.
There was just an empty space - a vast empty space – my world - as I knew it - had emptied.

I end this chapter with the words of the hymn that my sister and I chose for dad's funeral.
It is a hymn that meant a lot to dad:
It was the hymn that was sung at his father's funeral.
And - the hymn that was played by a band on the dock side; as his ship, carried his unit and himself away to Canada. Those young men - off to begin their RAF training - at the beginning of World War Two.

ABIDE WITH ME

Abide with me, fast falls the eventide;
The darkness deepens, Lord with me abide;
When other helpers fail, and comforts flee,
Help of the helpless, O abide with me.

Swift to its close ebbs out life's little day;
Earth's joys grow dim, its glories pass away;
Change and decay in all around I see:
O Thou who changest not, abide with me.

I need Thy presence every passing hour;
What but Thy grace can foil the tempter's power?
Who like Thyself my guide and stay to be?
Through cloud and sunshine, O abide with me.

I fear no foe, with Thee at hand to bless;
Ills have no weight, and tears no bitterness;
Where is death's sting? Where, grave thy victory?
I triumph still, if Thou abide with me.

Hold Thou Thy Cross before my closing eyes,
Shine through the gloom, and point me
to the skies;
Heaven's morning breaks, and earth's vain
shadows flee:
In life, in death, O Lord, abide with me.

Henry Francis Lyle 1793 - 1847

THE DAY THOU GAVEST

The day Thou gavest, Lord is ended,
The darkness falls at Thy behest;
To Thee our morning hymns ascended,
Thy praise shall sanctify our rest

We thank Thee that thy Church unsleeping.
While earth rolls onward into light,
Through all the world her watch is keeping.
And rests not now by day or night.

As o'er each continent and island
The dawn leads on another day,
The voice of prayer is never silent,
Nor dies the strain of praise away.

The sun that bids us rest is waking
Our brethren 'neath the western sky,
And hour by hour fresh lips are making
Thy wondrous doings heard on high.

So be it, Lord; Thy throne shall never,
Like earth's proud empires, pass away;
Thy kingdom stands, and grows for ever,
Till all Thy creatures own Thy sway.

John Ellerton 1826 - 1893

CHAPTER FIVE

GATHERING

1991

Mum and Dad had moved house twice since leaving the family home where my sister and I grew up and although I had helped them dispose of items they didn't need on both of these occasions, there were still many things to be sorted through – an entire lifetimes collection.

I found that entering the house was very sad, it felt empty, cold and quiet and yet it looked just the same - as if you had called when they were out, expecting that they would return just as the kettle had boiled - as per usual.

The only way for me to enter was to take a deep breath, shut everything else out, and concentrate on what I had come to do that particular day.

The refrigerator, important paper work and valuable items, were our starting point.

It was agreed, between my sister and I, that I would keep dad's wedding ring (he had previously given me an old signet ring of his) and mum's engagement ring.

For me, this ring held memories;

Memories of mum and I sitting together through all those church services when I was small:

When I got bored during the service (I would be four or five years old) I would reach across, and slowly turn her engagement ring around her finger, so that the two stones of the ring were pointing inwards. I would look up at Mum, and she in turn, would look down at me, with a look of feigned annoyance, on her face. Sometimes, it seemed to me, she hadn't noticed what I had done, and with some impatience, I would nudge her arm and point to her hand and grin.

Mum would leave the ring round that way, for an unspecified length of time, and then turn the ring the correct way round. Meanwhile, I would be watching and waiting, eager for the ring to be turned round, which was my cue to move the ring again. This game was similar to a game of chess, but without the aid of a clock.

Mum endured my repeated behaviour, showing exceptional patience and calmness, through many sermons and lesson readings.

Wearing this ring has not granted me those same qualities.

Items were shared between my sister and I - laid out to be chosen or discarded – one for you, one for me, one for the charity shop, and one for the dustbin.

I soon found myself taking home with me anything that was definitely not wanted by my sister.

All the old glassware that had been in Mum's family, including the little green dish that was brought out every Christmas to have nuts placed in it.

Glass cake stands (3 of).

Vases and books- including books that Dad had as a child.

The book case complete with all its contents – including the book in its cardboard box that was kept on the bottom shelf of the bookcase – "not to be touched by children".

In fact, as a child, I rarely handled any of the books – without firstly asking for permission.

It was only when I got this particular "boxed" book home, that I looked at it for the first time in my life, and then only after I had checked that I was alone. It was a medical book describing such things, (with pictures), as the difference between Measles and German Measles and how to spot "nettle rash".

I suppose it isn't all that strange to find, that years of being told to "leave that book alone" had had an effect on me and that as I opened its' cardboard box I felt like a naughty mischievous child.

About three years after I had taken possession of the bookcase and it's contents; Armon came to visit me:

"You've got my book," he said.

I was amazed and excited, and immediately rushed over to the bookcase to search for it. My search started with the hymnbooks and bibles. I was looking for Armons name on the fly covers but it was not there. Moving to the shelf which I thought contained books from Dad's childhood, I pulled out;

"Arthur Mee's – Golden Year – Over the hills and far away". An illustrated book, telling of the authors travels around the world. Travels which took him to France, Italy, Switzerland, Norway and Egypt.

Methodically, and turning every page, I found an inscription;

> "With love and best wishes Xmas 1926 to Armon
> from Grandma and Grandpa
> Be Good, Do Good, and good will come to you"

I can't tell you how thrilled I was to discover this inscription. As far as I know, this book is the only possession of Armon's that there is. And every time I hold it, I imagine him, (he would have been 10yrs old), excitedly reading about those "far away" and "exotic" places.

After my sister and I had agreed that I would keep the bookcase she asked me if I was going to keep all the books in it. "Oh yes" I said surprised at the thought of changing it.
"And are you going to replace that broken piece of glass in the bottom of the door?"
"Oh no, I'll leave it just as it is".
She appeared to be satisfied with that answer.

There was a vase that had once held flowers in London Road Methodist Church, along with a wooden box that contained the little star stamps and inkpad that had been used to mark our attendance cards at Sunday school. The Japanese tea set that my maternal Grandfather had somehow brought home, the wooden candle sticks that mum grew up with, along with those from my Dads family and the "potato knife". This instrument was very old and originally must have had a blade about 4 – 5 inches long, however, the years, and frequent sharpening had taken its' toll and now the blade was roughly about 1 and a bit inches long. I well remember peeling potatoes with it one day as a child (a good job "Aunty Batty" didn't see me as it was always kept very sharp) and inadvertently throwing it in the bin with the peelings, I remember the panic when it was discovered that the potato knife was missing, and the subsequent emptying of the dustbin (no rubber gloves then) and the triumph, not to mention the relief, when I found it. A quick wash and normality was restored.
I was briefly tempted to keep this knife but decided to just keep the memories instead! Unlike the wooden "boiler stick", which, legend has it, one day - when I

was about 2 years old - and for some undisclosed reason, I cornered my sister and hit her with it. I must stress that I have no memory of this - that is not the reason I kept it. The reason I kept it was - I remember using it as a boiler stick, and because of its usage and age, the end that is put in hot water, feels like velvet.

The boiler had long since gone, but I do remember that during the winter of 1962 or 1963, when there was a lot of snow and ice - and no water or electricity for a few weeks, that old boiler was brought into the kitchen and repeatedly filled with snow, which, when melted, provided water not only for us, but for Mr and Mrs Trelfa.

Because I had more free time than my sister, I took it upon myself to become "chief sorter" and I approached my mission in a very orderly fashion.
I would set myself goals for the day and not stop until they had been completed – including a visit to a charity shop and the "skips" – everything that had been sorted, had to have a final destination at the end of the day.
I can't say that I felt Mum and Dad around me whilst I was "sorting", in fact I believe that I probably blocked any contact that there might have been – I needed to be singular in my approach to this job of work.

As so often in life, it was the small things that I came across that would stop my momentum;

The letters Mum had kept, that I had written to her when she was in hospital when I was about 8yrs old.

The tiny fairy that had sat at the top of the Christmas tree ever since my sisters' first Christmas and now reclaimed by her. As I took one last look at the fairy, I remembered the Christmas that Mum had been in the Royal Devonshire hospital in Buxton: That tiny fairy had clung to the top of the tree, from mid December, until the end of March the following year. Dad, insisting, that the tree remain – until Mum came home.

The headdresses that my sister and I had worn when we were bridesmaids for a cousin of Dads – we were 5yrs and 10yrs old respectively.

The train tickets that took Mum and Dad to their Honeymoon in March 1943.

Ration books from the 2nd World War, (the gas mask was, and still is, kept in the bookcase)

There was Dad's large leather suitcase that he had used during the war.
The suitcase that had been stored under my bed, when I was in that bedroom with the circus wallpaper.
The suitcase that - my mother told me, long after I had left home - was the hiding place for all my Christmas presents!
No wonder I Never found them!
I Never thought of looking under my own bed, well - how many children would? – Did You?

The unburied cremation ashes of one of their dogs:
I remember walking round their garden with the urn in one hand and a trowel in the other, angry that they had left this job for me to do, not being able to make a decision as to where to bury them. My final choice was near the bird bath. As I made that decision I "saw" the photographs that had been taken of Mum and Dad each stood on their own by that bird bath - then, I decided to

take the bird bath home with me in case the new eventual owners of the house threw it out!

Dad's wooden door wedge!
Dad had worked as a chartered accountant for I C I.
The offices had fire doors across the corridors, which, at times, had to be momentarily held open in order for something to be moved through them. Ever prepared, my Dad always had a door wedge in his jacket pocket, a simple yet useful solution.
I had put the door wedge in the bookcase and one day John and I, having moved house, were positioning the bookcase. We realised that the floor was uneven. "What we need is a wedge", we said in harmony. I just opened the door of the bookcase and pulled out Dad's wedge.
You never know when you are going to need a door wedge! Thanks Dad.

The pink orthopaedic splints that had been made for Mum's hands as an aid to preventing their seizure, as Rheumatoid Arthritis took hold

The envelopes marked "screws" that Dad had methodically stored, not to mention his collection of paper clips and assorted rubber bands.

I systematically went through everything, displaying the items on the kitchen worktops ready for my sister to take the things she wanted. Following one of her visits to the house and while I was at home, the phone rang. Answering it, I heard a pinging noise coming down the receiver and the voice of my Brother in Law asking, "Do you know what this is? I'll do it again" "Ping" – it was the biscuit tin!
When we were children, there were two cylindrical metal biscuit tins with lids that made a " pinging" noise

when they were removed, one lid "pinged" louder than the other, and it always seemed to be that one which had the interesting biscuits like custard creams or chocolate in it. The plain Rich Tea biscuits were in the other one. This ruse meant that no matter how hard you tried, we were unable to "sneak" a chocolate biscuit, the "ping" always gave you away.

My sister and I have one tin each now and in mine I keep the dog's "Treat" biscuits and when the dog hears that "ping" she comes running.

As our back bedroom became more and more cluttered, Mum and Dad's house became emptier and colder, just an empty shell. I didn't want to be there any more.

The last thing to be dealt with was the television set, and my frustration with the Television Company, grew.

Mum and Dad had always rented their television and the company had been informed that the television was no longer required. We had agreed a mutual time for them to come to remove it, however, as so often happens, and for the second time - they didn't arrive.

Still it sat there, in the corner of the living room - like some immovable object.

"Couldn't these people understand how awful it was to be waiting in this empty shell?"

"Didn't they know what it felt like to be tied to a house by a television?"

My frustration and anger led me to bounce into their shop and demand that they

"COME and REMOVE IT" or else I would

"PUT IT IN THE CAR PORT and LEAVE IT THERE!"

This threat brought a warning "Oh I wouldn't do that – we would take a dim view of that action".

"WELL MOVE IT THEN".
A time was arranged again and I flounced out of the shop shaking and upset, but with my head held high, leaving in my wake shop assistants and customers who must have thought I was neurotic.

The last 10 months or so had obviously been stressful and it was a few months later, that John and I realised that over a 12 month period   - he had been to six funerals and I had been to five.
There was so much loss.

With the house empty and up for sale, I turned my attention to all the old paperwork that had been uncovered, and in order for my sister and I to share it, I began photocopying everything.
There were birth and death certificates, funeral notices and obituaries and articles from old local newspapers, pieces of the family history handed down thoughout the years.
In order to make some sense of all this information I began to place my copies in a folder in chronological order, with a place at the back for photographs.
My Family was in a blue folder.

Not long after Mum had died, I had begun to dream about her.
The dreams were nearly always the same; she was in her hospital bed – sometimes looking happy – sometimes sad, and I was stood at the foot of the bed – looking at her and waving "Goodbye", then I would wake up.

However, shortly after Dad had died, my Mum came to visit me:

One night as I was having a bath, Mum came in and shouted at me" *You've got to do something or you'll end up like me – Don't let anyone stop you – Do something"*

I was shocked, scared and very confused. She had never spoken to me like this before, I didn't understand the message, in fact I didn't understand anything.
These outbursts which only happened at night - when I was having my bath - became a regular nightly occurrence and along with the recurring dreams was very disturbing. I spent the next five months or so, unable to go to sleep, very often sitting in the living room until the early hours of the morning – waiting for the barrage of what felt like accusations, and believing that I would never be "normal" again. I felt as though I was going mad - or she was.

As the months went on Mum and Dad's house was sold.
John was the Executor of the Will and, as he returned to his car, (after a last visit to the solicitor where he signed the final papers,) he found that the car was full of the smell of pipe smoke. Dad had smoked a pipe for years and was now using this to let us know that he was near us. Brilliant!

I brought a car with some of the proceeds of the estate and I had a very strong urge to show it to Mum and Dad. I didn't understand this urge, I couldn't explain it, I KNEW Mum and Dad were around yet I still had to drive to the Crematorium to show them the car. The act of doing this only convinced me further - that indeed - I was going mad.

I drove to the Crematorium, parked the car and
followed the written notification to their plots. I easily
found the place.

Mum was on one side of a lawn – Dad was on the
opposite side

Handy for me, a bench had been placed on the path
facing the centre of the lawn and it was here I sat –
between them – and said "Hello – I've bought the car to
show you. Do you like it?"

I got no reply and no smell of pipe smoke so after a
couple of minutes I stood up to leave. "Thanks for the
car – I love it".

And with that said, I left.

The urge to visit all my family graves grew very fast
and very strong.

John was taking all this strange behaviour in his stride,
never once did he question what I was doing – I never
noticed him looking at me oddly, he just gave me the
space to be me and to carry out my missions and now I
was off on another one:

The joint grave of my paternal grandparents, which I
hadn't visited since my grandmother had died, was easy
to find as the graveyard was only a small one, and
having found it, I just stood there and said, "Hello – it's
me". Receiving no answer – I left.

The grave of my adopted Great Grandparents was more
difficult to find, as that particular churchyard had many
"old" graves in it. For some reason I chose a very wet
day for my search and hindsight tells me that if I had
bothered to "ask" for their help I wouldn't have got so
wet and cold. But I was on a mission and I felt that the
only way to find it was the "hard way". I had a need to

travel some kind of pilgrimage through that wet graveyard.

I started my quest at what looked like the oldest part, and worked my way along each row, being careful not to step on any grave of course, but still no sign. Getting nearer the Church itself I found that the graves were indeed very old and even worse than that, the path was made up of gravestones, and I had been walking over them.

I was beginning to think that I had missed their grave, and would have to start all over again, and so I stood still (dripping profusely) - to give myself a minute to review the situation.

Yes! You guessed correctly.

I found that I was stood directly in front of it and, not only that, the grave was adjacent to the main path which led directly to the Church doors. Common sense, would have told me to begin my search from there in the first place, but common sense eluded me.

The time that I had spent, the rain and the cold that I was suffering from, all contributed to the sense of achievement that I felt.

I was surprised to see that not only were my "grandparents" buried there, but their son and daughter and a gentleman who had died in 1916 during the Battle of Jutland.

Again I stood at the foot of the grave and said with great satisfaction,

"I've found you – hello it's me".

Again I heard no reply and so I walked with as much dignity as my soggy state would allow, back to my car and drove home.

I felt triumphant and as soon as I got home I wrote down the directions to the grave in my blue folder.

I had visited the grave of my maternal Grandparents'
and my Uncle Armon once before, at the request of
Dad. One day he had quietly asked John and I to go and
see if the grave was alright, as apparently, Mum had
been talking about it but couldn't bring herself to visit.
"There's a tree by it" were our directions and so we set
off to the parish Church to seek it out.

The trees were planted alongside the paths and
eventually we did find the grave by a Holly tree and
reported back that, "It was alright"
Now a few years later as I was on my mission, I read an
article in the local paper in which the Church were
asking for family members of those interred, to go
along to check the graves, as there had been a bout of
vandalism and some old grave stones had been pushed
over.

I scurried along as soon as I could and reported to the
"groundsman". He asked me which grave I had come to
see, and checked the details in his ledger.
He repeated the names of my Grandparents and my
Uncle and then said – "name only".
"What do you mean – name only" I asked.

"Well your Uncles body is not in the grave, his name
has been added to the headstone"

I was stunned. "Where was Armon, why just his
name?" I just couldn't understand why this should be.
"Why had nobody told me – what was going on?"

I now embarked on another mission, I was upset at this
news and I HAD to find out where Armon was.

Armon had been in the Army during the 2nd World War and had been taken prisoner by the Japanese – he didn't survive the ordeal – and that was all I knew.

Armed with this information and a photograph of Armon in army uniform, I went to see a neighbour of ours who was very interested in Military history.

He amazed me with the amount of information that he gave me there and then.

He told me the name of Armons' regiment, where they had served, adding, that Armon and his unit, had been captured by the Japanese on the island of Java, only 2 days after landing on it.

I was staggered by this information but I needed to know more.

Our neighbour suggested that I get in touch with a man called Mr Tomkinson of the local Royal British Legion and he gave me his telephone number.

Mr Tomkinson was a very nice man who took the only details that I had, which amounted to a name and now a regiment and said "Well I'll see what I can do, but I can't promise you anything".

A few weeks later Mr Tomkinson rang to say that he had some information and he asked if he could he come to see me.

I didn't know what to expect as Mr Tomkinson handed me an envelope, and I felt nervous, excited and upset all at the same time.

"If you would like to open the envelope after I have gone that's fine" he said.

"Oh no – I'll open it now" I said trying to smile.

The first letter from the Graves Commission spoke about a person called William Armon and I remember thinking "This isn't him, it's the wrong person" and my heart sank, I had only ever heard him referred to as Armon, but at the bottom of the letter it named William Armon's parents and wife (as next of kin) – my Grandparents and Auntie!

They had found Armon.

There was another letter from the Graves Commission and then the most surprising of all – a letter from Jefferson Barracks National Cemetery, St Louis. USA. And not only a letter, but also, two photographs of Armons' grave.
Armon had been taken to America.

Without going into too much detail, Mr Tomkinson explained how the Americans, who had liberated the camp, would then be responsible for those that they found there. These freed prisoners were placed onto American ships, and taken to America.
Mr Tomkinson went on to say, that it appeared to be the case, that Armon had still been alive when the camp was liberated, but had died a short while after. He was 29yrs old.

A few years after being given this information, I asked Armon one day, if the information was correct.
Armon confirmed that he had been alive when the Americans came, adding that he had relinquished the responsibility for his survival to them – exhaustion and relief, overcoming him.

I felt as though I couldn't express my gratitude to Mr Tomkinson sufficiently, he wanted no payment, he was genuinely pleased to help, and pleased that he had a result, as that is not always the case as he had first warned me.

I have sometimes wondered how many missions Mr Tomkinson undertook.

I wrote to the Royal British Legion (enclosing a donation) and to the Graves Commission and to Jefferson Barracks to express my gratitude - although words didn't seem to be enough. If it had not been for their care in keeping all the records, I would never have had this information.
I take this opportunity to thank Mr Tomkinson and these three organisations again in these pages.
Thank You.

When I had visited the grave of my Grandparents' following the report in the paper, the Groundsman had come with me, and on finding that the headstone was beginning to fall over, we agreed that in order for it to be preserved, it should be laid down on top of the grave.
The work would be carried during the next few weeks, free of charge.
There were two urns on the grave and I decided against burying them as and been suggested, and took them home with me. I felt responsible for them, burying them felt like discarding them-there was no way I could let that happen.

I still have those urns, unfortunately one is now broken and on reflection, it would probably have been wise to bury them, but I was gathering – not discarding.

There was one more loss that year:

NOVEMBER 1991.

Muppet, our Bearded Collie, used to sleep at the top of the stairs and one morning in late November he didn't get up as he heard us stirring. This was very unusual as he was the type of dog that would jump up in expectation, having read your mind - knowing before you did, that you would soon be going to do something and he was going to "help".

It was obvious that he was very unwell and so we called the vet.

John had an appointment to keep and so had to leave.

During the time between John leaving and the vet arriving, Muppet was fading fast. It was like watching my Dad disappearing – I felt helpless and very scared that Muppet would die before the vet arrived and whilst I was alone with him. I wasn't aware of any Spirit who had come to help; there was just Muppet and me.

I knelt with him and spoke to him but hardly got a response, he was deaf and had cataracts and now I was watching his life was just ebbing away.

The vet arrived, late morning and Osmart Black Panther – aged 14 ½ yrs – was put to sleep.

CHAPTER SIX

UN–FOLDING

During the period of 1992 and early 1993 I was listening to my music more and more. Playing a series of differing mood music during each session – as previously described.

Dreams were very much a feature of my sleeping hours.

- Mum in her hospital bed – sometimes happy – sometimes sad.
- I'm in a house, it is war time and soldiers are shooting into the house, I have no escape.
- I'm in a railway station – "Where is the ticket office?" I can't find it – I can't find the correct platform – I can't get on the train. I have no ticket.

All these were recurring dreams and one night whilst dreaming again of the war time house, I was not alone inside it, John was with me.

When I related this latest dream to John the next morning he told me that he had had a similar dream that night as well.

Things were starting to get more confused.

As I understand now, the Universe works in a wondrous way, and it was in the summer of 1993 that a friend and work colleague of ours told us that, through the course of his work, he had interviewed a Medium and Spiritual Healer, and he invited us to attend the Civic Hall in Winsford, Cheshire one evening, as they were giving a talk on Healing and a session of Mediumship.

There were quite a number of people in the audience that night and I expect that like 99% of them I hoped to receive a message – surely "They" wouldn't waste the opportunity to speak to me, to explain why my mother was "haunting" me, to tell me what the future held - my belief at this time, being that my life had lost it's purpose.

And so I sat there pretending to be nonchalant, trying not to fidget in my seat, and trying not to care if indeed, I didn't get a message.

Tracy, the medium, did point to John and I and said, "they say things are going to be better", that was our message.

After the evening finished John and I were introduced to Tracy and her partner Jon and it was then that Tracy said to me – "you will get what you want".

Well, this threw me into a panic.

I had been feeling lost and sorry for myself and had stupidly said in conversations with myself, "if I have no useful purpose left in my life – then I may as well not be here".

Now here was Tracy giving me this message - did they mean that I was going to die?

"When they say get what you want, what do they mean? I asked.

"Things will be better" came back the reply.

"Oh good". Well that was alright then wasn't it!

The next thing I knew was that John was arranging to go and meet with Tracy and Jon. When I asked her when I could go, she said, "I'll ask them and see what they say" and with that they disappeared to speak to other people.

Just when I was beginning to think that Tracy had forgotten my request, she reappeared and said. "'I've asked them and they said that you can come and see me in nine weeks".

NINE WEEKS! Why on earth did I have to wait NINE WEEKS!
John was going to see them in a few days time.
This was NOT FAIR – why make ME wait for NINE WEEKS!

To say that the nine weeks went slowly would be putting it mildly and to add insult to injury John was having an amazing time.
His, is not my story to tell - suffice it to say that he gained a lot of understanding about things that had happened throughout his life and learning how he could further use his healing energies.

As my nine weeks drew to and end I arranged to meet Tracy for a sitting, during which, my Dad and Mum came and one of the things that was mentioned was that I would write a book.

"No way" was my reaction to that one.

Tracy also told me that there was someone within my energy field, my aura, who wanted to put me "On the right path" and she also said, that Muppet was with them all.

So all in all I had confirmation that Mum and Dad and others were around me and that Muppet was well and happy.

I had no explanation for the dreams or as to why Mum was ordering me to *"Do something"* – but I did take comfort from a lot of things Tracy told me and when I told Jon about my sessions with my music, he explained to me about chakras in the body and how they vibrated. He also explained how we hold onto different emotions within these chakras. I now understood why the music made me happy or sad and I was very soon to discover how Spirit would use music to communicate with me, and to assist me in communicating with them.

It was shortly after this reading that a strange event occurred.

John and I had just got into bed and were both beginning to fall asleep when simultaneously we sat up with a jump and both said in harmony – "an Eagle has just landed on the bottom of the bed!"

The huge Eagle then flew away.

We were amazed and puzzled but we both felt and believed that he or she had come to protect us both and guide us on our "paths".

Since that event we have noticed other instances when, if we have been out walking, a single bird has hovered above us and led the way home and on a very recent occasion a flock of birds surrounded our car whilst we were driving along a country road. As we slowed down to avoid the swooping birds we realised that up through the trees to our right hand side was a house that we had been looking for.

If it hadn't been for the birds we would have gone past the property.

Now, the reason that I dropped History at the end of my third year in Secondary school, was that I couldn't remember dates. It was of no interest to me when Henry viii reigned or indeed in what order he married his six wives (it was six wasn't it?") and so it was with this same brainpower that I entered into this world of Spirit learning.

I would say to John "what's that "sh" word? Tell me again"
"Chakra" he would say, and explain what it was.

"Oh right – and they spin do they?"
" Should they spin in a certain direction?"

It was getting too complicated for me, and so I decided to forget all that and have a go - my own way.

My way, was to sit - my eyes closed - with my music and "feel" it penetrate parts of my body, and one day as I was doing this I saw the colour Pink.

"I saw Pink today" I reported and John explained once more, how each chakra had a colour linked to it.
I was very enthused and continued to watch for more colours with eager anticipation.

John had also mentioned something else that he had learned - and that was - raising your vibrations.
Somewhere inside me this phrase resonated and so I began to sit with my music and repeat the words – "I wish to raise my vibrations and I know that somewhere inside me, I know how to do this".

So there I would sit, repeating this phrase and waiting for something to happen.

I must mention at this point that John and I had closed our picture framing business in order to embark on a partnership into another business and so I was no longer working five days a week and was now at home. This gave me lots of time and space to devote to developing what skills I could, in order to see if I could improve my communication with the Spirit world.

Very soon I was aware of my Mum, I could not only see her, but I could feel her vibrating in front of me, a feeling akin to static electricity. She looked just the same as I remembered her only she was well and smiling.
Just as I got used to recognising Mum around, I felt another "someone" and it wasn't until I smelt the pipe smoke that I knew it was Dad.
I was learning that each visitor had a different vibration and as I was continuing to ask for my vibrations to be raised, I began to see little bits of them – my Dads lower legs - still clad in his favourite brown trousers - and Mum's face.

Now I could also feel something happening inside me – like a fluttering in different parts of my body.
I felt things were going very well and now I could talk briefly to Mum and Dad when they came, and so I decided to ask Tracy if I could see her again. It was now early November 1993, approximately two months after my first reading with her.

In preparation for going to see Tracy I pulled out a postcard that I had found when sorting through Mum and Dad's things.
This postcard had been posted to them two days after my birth.

On one side of the card - a picture of a face, peeping over a brick wall had been drawn, with the words "What no tenors?" written on it. Obviously a reference to me being a second daughter, but the thing that really puzzled me was the handwriting of the address looked just like my handwriting.

And the other amazing thing was that as I held the card in the palm of my hand, it would suddenly curl up, almost completely in on itself. I had given this card to John to hold and no matter how long he held it, only the edges would move – a tiny amount.

So it was that I set off to see Tracy with the card in my handbag and during the reading I asked her to ask "them" about the card.

The answer came back - that it was written by Mum's brother Arthur.

I demonstrated to Tracy just what happened when I held it and she held it herself and yet again there was only slight movement around the edges.

No explanation was given for this phenomena so I decided that I must "have a go" at dowsing in order to get answers to my questions.

Dowsing was something John had spoken of and so, determined to get some answers myself; when I arrived home from seeing Tracy, I and went in search for something to use as a suitable pendulum.

I knew you could dowse with rods and crystals but I supposed, that as long as it dangled, anything would work. So it was with great satisfaction that I decided that my pendulum would be my green plastic apple core complete with cord – an artefact that I had worn along with a small bell on a cord, with great pride in the seventies - well it was fashionable at the time!

I was now finding that I was seeing more colours when I listened to music – felt more tingling in and around my body – I was seeing blue darting lights, flitting around the room – smelling different aromas - on one occasion I heard Muppet walking around upstairs, (there was no doubt in my mind that the noise was Muppet, inwardly I recognised the vibration of his footsteps) – I was catching glimpses of Spirit out of the corner of my eye. Things were very exciting.

One evening John and I went again to see Tracy and Jon on stage, this time at the Parr Hall in Warrington.

During the evening they explained that they would both doing an exercise to expand their auras and they asked that the audience to report back on, what, if anything - they saw.
A "hush" spread around the room, as Jon and Tracy stood on the stage, in preparation for the exercise.
They remained standing – with their eyes closed, for several minutes.
Then, Tracy opened her eyes, and asked us if we had noticed anything.
Several people put their hands in the air and were invited to tell everyone what they had seen. The room began to fill with the buzz of murmured conversations, as people swapped stories with their neighbour.
I kept quiet because I had seen no colours and - to my annoyance - I had been distracted by someone coming noisily into the gallery above me.
Using this distraction and my subsequent lack of concentration as an excuse for my failure to see colours, I spoke to Tracy afterwards.
I related the story of the banging door adding, that unfortunately I hadn't seen any colours like the other

people, merely the moving shadows on the wall behind them both.

She looked at me and said "Well, no one came through that door and that was Spirit that you saw moving around – you have heard and seen Spirit".

I felt silly that I hadn't realised what had been happening but I was pleased to have the experience that night.

Just when I was used to seeing the blue darting lights around the room, I was thrown into a minor panic when I began to see brown ones. "What could these be?"
I felt that I must begin to use the apple core (A/C) in order to get the answer.
I understood that the A/C would swing one way for a yes answer and another way for a no answer, so with this meagre information, I sat with A/C and said, "Give me a yes". I watched in amazement as it slowly began to swing from North to South - gathering speed as it swung.

"Oh it's working," I thought with great excitement. "Give me a No," I demanded.

To my astonishment A/C slowed down and gradually began to swing from East to West. I repeated the exercise a few times – just to make sure it remained the same.
I believed that I now had the tools to answer all my questions - my communication with Mum and Dad, my A/C and Jon and Tracy.

The answer to the question of the brown lights Tracy told me, was Earth Elementals. This was confirmed by

A/C. My only understanding of what an Earth Elementals were, was that they were little elves and fairies who lived in the garden. I knew that they existed, because I had seen one in the garden. I had caught a quick glimpse of it's little legs as it ran out from behind the bird bath and disappeared round the back of the shed.

I felt happy that they were choosing to visit, but what I didn't understand, was why they were in the living room.

As a child I had always collected stones and shells if I was on a beach, or acorns and fir cones, if in a wood and I would take them home to build my collection. John had always collected fossils as a child and interesting stones like "Blue John" which comes from the "Blue John" mine in Derbyshire and together our interest in crystals began to grow. It was during this unfolding time, that I realised that when I held a stone or crystal, I could feel a vibration from it. At the time I thought of this as no more than another amazing thing that was happening – just something else to experience. I would learn more about their power in the future.

My Mum urged me to listen to more music and it was on one wonderful Sunday that I was drawn to put my tape "Moonlight Shadows" by the Shadows, into the player. As I listened one phrase from each track kept running through my mind

I turned the volume up and sat down to listen - asking that my vibrations be lifted. I was feeling the usual flutterings and the session went like this:

- **Track 10: "Three Times a Lady"**

"Hello Mum". She moves in closer. I can feel the energy of her.
I can feel her breathing in my face. The tears begin to fall slowly down my face.

 Three times a lady... Three times a lady.

"Who is three times a lady?"
"You are"

 Three times a lady... Three times a lady.

"What do you mean?"
"You are like your great grandmother – the Quaker".
"Great Grandma was a Quaker?"
"You are like her – three times a lady"
The love around me is too much. I am sobbing, smothered in their love.
I continue to sob.

- **Track 12: "I Just Called To Say I Love You"**

 I Just Called... I Just Called

Their love gets stronger – more overwhelming.
I can feel many around me, reaching out with their love – touching me.

- **Track 15: "Imagine"**

 Imagine all the people…

"I can feel you. Oh thankyou for coming. Thankyou for being there."

 Imagine all the people…

"I can feel you."

I sob until I can sob no more.

I need a cup of tea, a tissue and a cigarette!
Having pulled myself together I returned to listen to the music. Instantly, I am aware of different Spirits.

> *"This is my father – your Granddad"*
> "Oh Granddad, Oh hello, it's me"
>
> *"This is my mother – your Grandmother"*
> "Oh Grandma, hello"
>
> I'm crying again – quietly, and now I feel very hot, very, very hot! "OH WHAT IS THIS?"
> *"Your great Grandfather – Peter Joseph"*
> "Oh I'm so hot, he's coming for me, it's so hot"
> Peter: *"You will remember – when you feel the heat, you will know I am with you"*

I need another cup of tea and two cigarettes – and I must put the roast potatoes in the oven.
The meal is nearly ready and the music plays on.

I'm staggered at what has happened today. My family came to visit.

I'll just sit down and think about it all.

> "Oh there's an old lady, I can feel her moving closer. It's an old lady"
>
> *"OLD LADY - HOW RUDE – HOW VERY RUDE"*
>
> "Oh I'm sorry – oh dear – you are Great Grandma?"
>
> *"How rude you are – no manners!"*
>
> "Hello, I'm sorry, hello".
>
> *"How rude"*

And she disappears.

I must make the gravy. I'm sorry Great Grandma!

This was truly an amazing afternoon.

Reflecting on it, some time later, I realised how beneficial it had been for me.

I understood the lesson they were teaching me;

They chose a time of day when part of my brain was aware of the practical things I had to do, in this case, cooking a meal.

Knowing how excited I was to receive their communication, they knew that I would automatically learn to hold some of that higher vibration whist dashing in and out of the kitchen.

I was beginning to learn to maintain some level of higher vibration, whilst doing ordinary things, returning to raise my levels - which had inevitably dropped - as I sat again.

This was a very valuable early lesson for me in raising vibrations. I have learnt that raising your vibrational level is a never ending quest – I know that the body remembers the last level achieved – I know that continual expansion of vibrational levels is required for our health, and certainly for clear communication.

I occasionally heard Dad mooching around.

He was one of those people who would move around the house, look out of a window, look in a drawer, pick up a book, go back to the window, not doing or looking for anything in particular – just mooching. (I mooch a lot now, much to the exasperation of the dog, who will occasionally mooch behind me).

Anyway, Dad would mooch around the bookcase and sometimes I would hear the door shut.

I would say "Hi" to him and I would always feel particularly emotional when Dad was around.

One day he followed me into the living room and said.

"Put Chris Rea on"

"Chris Rea – how have you heard of Chris Rea?"

I could feel his insistence as I tried to question him again and so I found my Chris Rea tape and noticed that it had been played only half way through.

I had realised by now that there was always a message in the music that I was requested to play, be it a mood, a single word or a sentence, but always a message, and so I asked Dad "Which way round shall I put the tape in?"

"The other way round" was my instruction.

The track that began was "I want to be with you" and this was followed by "Tell me there's a heaven".

Dad and I listened to the tracks together, my sobbing, nearly drowning out the sound coming from the player.

I always seemed to be crying - but they were tears of happiness.

One day Dad came and as I sat down to "tune in" to him, I saw that there was a woman, slightly older than myself, with him.

"This is your sister – this is Megan," said Dad.

Feelings of shock and amazement rushed through me as Dad went on to explain how Megan had grown up in the spirit world (mum having mis-carried her).
N.B. Later during my development, I would learn more about how children grew up within the Spirit world. How they are nurtured. How they are able to develop at whatever rate is right for them. How, in some instances, some of them can "age" – instantaneously.
As I looked at Megan, and as we both said "Hello", I could sense that she was more like my physical sister in nature, than I was; quietly spoken and much more "lady–like".
It was an incredible meeting and "Oh" how I wished that my sister had been there to meet Megan.

Granddad's pendulum clock was hanging on the wall in the dining room but because of it's erratic time keeping I had stopped winding it up.
One day I realised that it was ticking and so I went and stood in front of it - wondering why it was going. I knew I hadn't wound it up and I also knew that John wouldn't have done as he had told me that just as in my Grandparents day, "there could be only one winder" and that was me.
As I was standing there, I smelt the now familiar pipe smoke.
"Hello Dad – the clocks started". I said.
I was immediately aware that someone else had come with him so I went and sat down to work on my vibrations in order to communicate – A/C was near by.

As I sat, eyes closed, I knew I was in the presence of someone different.

> "Granddad?"
>
> *"I've seen the clock"*
>
> "It's going, have you done that? – it won't keep time, what's wrong with it?"
>
> *"You will know when it likes a house because it will keep good time"*
>
> "Thankyou for coming – thankyou for bringing him Dad"

They left.

The clock continued ticking for about an hour and a half and then it stopped.

I was having a brilliant time – I was buzzing.

I had been visited by my family; I could talk to them and hear their reply.

Little lights were flashing around the house.

The bad dreams were fading, although they were replaced by a myriad of other equally confusing ones.

I was sleeping and talking happily whilst asleep, to the extent that on some mornings when I awoke, I felt as though I had been working all night long, having had no rest at all.

I felt very excited - and - well – just buzzing.

John and I would visit with Tracy and Jon quite often and it was during one of these visits that Jon said that I must be "Grounded". He explained that it was very important for us all to be connected to the earth if we were working with Spirit energy.

Jon came and crouched down in front of me; "Just imagine tree roots, coming up from the ground, and attaching themselves to your feet"

As I sat with Jon's hand on my feet I felt more than a little embarrassed. Nonetheless, as I shut my eyes and

concentrated, I began to see white roots snaking around and across my feet. I felt the ground tugging at my feet.
When he had completed the task, he advised me to sit still for a couple of minutes, adding, that I might be a little dizzy or that I might find that my legs felt a bit "heavy".
He was right – although I felt "normal" – when I tried to stand – I fell back into my seat - it took several minutes for normality to be restored.

The thing that staggered me more than anything, was, as I looked at Jon, just as he had finished the grounding, I felt a personal connection with him, almost a feeling that Jon and I had "found" one another. I felt as though he knew and understood everything about me.
Feeling very uncomfortable with this thought, and aware that Tracy and John were watching, I took a deep breath and said;
"Right, let me say this while we are all sitting here" – turning to Jon, I said, "Jon I feel some strange connection to you, I don't understand what has happened".
Jon explained, that through the shared channelled energy, I had felt this connection, but that the connection was with the Spirit world and not with him as an individual.
That explanation resonated with me and having mentioned it there and then, in front of John and Tracy, I wouldn't be going home with some distorted view of what had happened or feelings of guilt.
What a relief!

Over the years, I have been made aware of these "connection" feelings – experienced by others and I know that some people have become confused because of them:

If these feelings are not openly discussed, diffused and understood – between the people concerned - it can lead to fantasy, disillusionment and inevitably – upset, anger and loneliness. And in some cases – years wasted, in the belief that the one you have connected with will eventually realise the "connection" themselves and that - eventually – you will both "ride off into the sunset" together.

Understand – that yes – we link spiritually – with those around us – that is what we as supposed to do.
Do not – use that link – as an escape – or – as an excuse to stop yourself from dealing with relationship issues that already exist in your life.

On the 6th January 1994 as I was taking the Christmas decorations down, I felt Mum arrive.
Christmas can be a very emotional time for a lot of people – a time when the pain of losing someone, is felt more keenly, and John and I were no exception.
Feeling the loss of both our Mum's and my Dad, it was with them in our thoughts, that we decorated our house at Christmas. The tree is especially significant, as in previous years – since we were married, John and had had always bought three Christmas trees – one for his Mum and Dad, one for mine, and one for ourselves, and we had always potted them and decorated them as well, and yes – on the 6th of January we did it all in reverse. So when I became aware of Mum that day, I felt as though she was saying thankyou on behalf of them all.

Musically, I had now discovered the haunting sound of Pan Pipes, and the amazing sound quality of the CD rather than an audiotape and I had begun to add these to my collection.

"Moonlight Shadows" was now being played on our new CD player, with the added bonus of being able to select the track of your choice - an absolute delight for me, as I could repeat tracks at will.

John had bought me my own piano and an electronic keyboard some years earlier and I still enjoyed playing them for my own amusement - I noted in the diary, that I had begun to keep, that I was particularly drawn to play on the 19th 20th and 21st of January 1994.

On the 22nd of January, as I was sat listening to a new Pan Pipe CD, I heard the front door close and at the same time; I began to feel apprehensive and very excited, all rolled into one.

I sat in my armchair, tensing and unable to move, I knew a Spirit had entered the house and I knew something was going to happen.

I didn't know who the Spirit was; I was so full of excited apprehension and anticipation that I was unable to tune in. All I could do was to sit and wait for whatever it was that was going to happen.

What I didn't feel – was fear.

The haunting track "Bilitas" was playing, as the Spirit grew nearer. The energy was overwhelming and forced me further back into the chair, my vibrations immediately began to lift, higher and higher – higher than anything I had achieved before – I was buzzing.

The Spirit continued to move slowly towards me, stronger and ever nearer, it continued on and walked straight through me and out of the back of the chair.

My heart was thumping and racing as the Spirit left the house, closing the front door with a bang, announcing its departure.

As I began to calm myself, I realised that I knew this energy, it felt familiar – it was Armon, my mothers' brother.

Still reeling from the power of his energy, I reached for A/C and asked the question that I already knew the answer to – "Was that Armon?"
A/C said, "Yes".

I was thrilled and amazed by what he had done, it was brilliant - HE WALKED STRAIGHT THROUGH ME! My whole being was quivering, my breathing was rapid, the palms of my hands were sweating, even the chair felt as though it too, was vibrating beneath me.

Armon began to visit very often, and, having enjoyed the experience of him walking through me, and of him, "Knocking my socks off" on that occasion - I continued to play the tune "Bilitas" in the hope that it would happen again.

However, he chose to announce his presence by suddenly leaping out in front of me – wearing a blue shirt, dark trousers and a huge smile, and saying –
"Hiya kid".

CHAPTER SEVEN

GATHERING SPEED

The last five months had been a whirlwind of amazing experiences and events, and being someone who had their feet very much "on the ground", and not wanting to be lost in confusion, I felt it necessary to begin noting down the differing sensations I felt when visited by a particular Spirit energy.

I also needed to understand who was my guide and who was my doorkeeper, as my doorkeeper had changed from one grandfather (Granddad William) to my other Grandfather (Granddad William John – who had been known as Jack). The different sensations could be very confusing and I felt that I needed clarification and regular up-dates.

For example;
Mum – cold down my spine. (guide)
Dad – the smell of pipe smoke or the bookcase door being opened or closed. (guide)
Great-granddad (Peter Joseph) – great heat which filled the room. A very powerful presence.
Armon – "Hiya kid", or the noise of the front door closing. (A guiding light for all of my life)
The smell of lavender wood polish is a smell connected to my maternal grandmother.
Granddad William. A recognisable presence. One who had watched over me all my life.
Granddad Jack. The ticking clock. Another watcher all my life.
Mum in law – Elsie. Usually laughing and joking. The smell of Menthol sweets - although I have no

recollection of her using them - but it is a very distinctive smell.

Feeling as though someone was breathing in my face or moving the hair on top of my head.

Feeling a sudden draught.

Seeing or hearing movement to the side of me.

All these sensations were enhanced with my inner recognition of their unique vibrational energy,
my own emotions and a visual awareness.

I had begun to ask for distant healing for people – both those that I knew, and those that I did not.

This came about after a brief discussion on the subject with Tracy and Jon on one of our weekly visits - which invariably ended in the early hours of the morning.

But my real motivation was – seeing a News item on the television, which featured the plight of a young boy who lay seriously ill in hospital, with a mysterious illness.

It appeared that the boys illness was baffling medical science, the boy's condition was worsening and his parents were desperate for help as they feared they would lose him.

And so I began a nightly routine of sitting, asking Granddad to protect me, followed by a request for distant healing for anyone who I thought would benefit from it – using their names where possible or, if I didn't know a name, I would say "for that woman who I saw on the news – you know who I mean" – I trusted that "they" knew who I was talking about.

I also believed that there would be other people who would be motivated in the same way.

N.B. Many months later I happened to see an article about this child and his family. It explained how the boy had suffered from a baffling illness, had been very close to death, and was now recovering well – beyond all expectation.
It seemed to me – to be a miracle.

I had quickly realised that Spirit were around all the time – just waiting to pop in and speak. I also realised that I had no hiding place – not even the bathroom.
Just as my mother had come when I was in the bath, so, someone would drop in to say something to me whilst I was sitting on the toilet.
I found this embarrassing at first, but over the years – well - it's just become normal happening.

The act of bathing is a good way for me to cleanse my aura and invariably I will work in the early hours of the morning – after a bath.

Returning to the subject of my nightly requests for distant healing - which I had now begun to write down, I thought that now would be a good time to give you a few examples to show how quite unremarkable, from my perspective, they were – so here I go:

20th December 1993.
Opened up for distant healing (did list). Got emotional, felt Armon briefly. Will wait for confirmation.
A/C says it was Armon.

24th December1993.
Opened up for distant healing (did list). John felt heat and so did I. Thought I heard a pendulum clock ticking.

31st December 1993.
Opened up for distant healing (did list). Chest felt tight. John's mum Elsie came to say hello and "Happy New Year".

7th January 1994.
Opened up for distant healing (did list). I saw the usual purple – lots of it. Saw blue and green.

11th January 1994.
Opened up for distant healing (did list). Heard a thumping noise. Heard Muppet on the stairs.

I continued to write accounts of any dreams that I remembered, and also began to add those happenings that I believed to be significant to my development. One such happening reads as follows: -

12th January 1994.
As I was sat in a café in Llandudno, North Wales, I suddenly felt a pain in my stomach and back.
I overheard one waitress say to another "Oh, my stomach still aches".
I asked for some distant healing for her.
As the waitress walked away – the pain left me.

It was apparent to me that all the work I was continuing to do with my vibrations was making me more sensitive to the energy of other people. Like many other people, I had often been able to sense the "tension in the air", left in a room, after some one had had an argument – but now I noticed, that I was feeling the tension of the person.

This was brilliant – an opportunity for me to ask for help for someone.

Of course, I was fortunate that the pain left me as I asked for help.
I was fortunate that my family were guiding, teaching and protecting me.

Another example of sensing a person's energy was: -
One evening when John and I were at a social evening at Tracy and Jon's, I found myself sitting opposite a young man who, I noticed, had been very quiet all night.
As the evening wore on and as he seemed to become more morose, I said to him, "You look fed up".
He explained that he had had an argument with someone earlier that day and had now developed a headache.
Hearing our conversation, Tracy said to him "give Lynn your watch and see what she "gets"".
As soon as I held the watch (that's psychometry), I began to experience the anger that he was feeling following his argument.
I instinctively crossed my legs and tensed my muscles – his anger was intensifying.

As this energy was pouring into me I heard someone in the room "helpfully" suggest that I "uncross my legs and put my feet flat on the floor" (a typical meditation pose). Just in the nick of time – before I could un-tense my muscles to reply to her – I heard Tracy say "Leave her, and watch".

With my concentration now fully on receiving this energy, I looked to the man and quietly said "keep sending it to me".

His anger surged across the room – through my body – and exited through the back of my chair.
This episode lasted for several minutes.

The intensity of the energy began to wane and I began to unfurl – then it was over.

"Thank you – I feel much better – my headache has gone" he said.

"It's a pleasure" was my bemused reply.

The social evening continued.

Later that night and back at home, I asked Armon for an explanation of what had happened.
He explained that, simply – I had been willing and capable of receiving the man's energy and filtered it harmlessly through my aura, thus facilitating a Healing.
It was at this point that I realised that I hadn't asked for any protection, nor had the thought crossed my mind that it might not be a wise idea to blindly take that watch, without firstly having some understanding what I was going to do with it.

Again, I was fortunate that I was being looked after.

Two dreams followed shortly afterwards: -

> **22nd/23rd January 1994.**
> I was learning about noise and vibration.
> I was with a man who was showing me that – if you touched a rock, it creates a sound, which, as it travels and reaches another object – the sound can be heard – but – the sounds are different as the vibrations change.

It is important to note that he only touched the rock – he didn't hit it.

It made a lovely sound – not like anything I had heard before.

I think I was humming the notes.

28th/ 29th January 1994.

I remember talking to someone about physical – soul – spirit bodies.

I felt the effect of splitting up – not whole.

Then coming together again.

I said "I feel weak" and somebody said – "well, you will, because you have not got your spirit".

It was difficult to walk about.

The person said "now put your spirit back and you will feel better".

I did.

I think I did this experiment more than once.

On the evening of 31st January 1994. John and I received a phone call from Tracy.

She and Jon had just moved into a new house and Tracy found that the energy in it was very oppressive. She explained that she had asked a few people to go along that evening to assist, by means of sharing their energy, in the cleansing of the property, and would we come and help.

We agreed to go but I felt the need to prepare for the visit, and so I sat and asked for my family to protect and help us all.

John and I arrived at 10.15pm – the last to arrive. The atmosphere was decidedly tense, and people were unusually quiet. Tracy asked us to follow her into the kitchen whilst she made us a drink. There she explained that, between them, she and Jon had discovered that there were 2 adults and 10 children "stuck" in the house. She then went on to say that the children were victims of sexual abuse, dating back many years, and that the adults had been the abusers.

There were eight of us present that night, seated in a circle and before we began the session – we all agreed to ask our guides to take the "stuck" spirits to the light.
We began, on Tracy's instruction, to pass energy round between ourselves.
Suddenly Tracy began to cough and splutter and then choke, it was obvious that spirit had moved into her energy field and we realised that Tracy was re–enacting the suffering of one of the children. She looked as though she was struggling to free herself from someones' grip, she was murmuring and flaying her head around and all the time, she was coughing.
It was very unpleasant.
I think it is correct to say that all of us were feeling very tense at this point and it wasn't until Tracy began to recover, and Jon confirmed, via his pendulum, that the child had gone "to the light".

The tension around the circle began to ebb and, feeling the need to recover from the unpleasant experience, we had a tea and cigarette break.
During this interval, Tracy asked if I would sit next to her when we resumed, as Jon had told her that the white light we had all asked for, appeared to emanate from my direction.

This time, as we sat down, I started to feel a tingling sensation in my feet.
Another child came close to Tracy – and was released.

Now, Jon's pendulum told him that all the other children and one adult (a woman) had been released at the same time.

At this point in the proceedings, the tingling sensation in my feet became stronger and started to creep up my legs.
The male adult spirit now moved very close to Tracy, and Tracy struggled to speak. She managed to tell us that he was very strong - and was trying to posses her.
She needed another break.
During this break, Tracy announced that someone was going to introduce themselves to us and as she said that, I felt Armon's presence come closer to me.

We all sat down again and once more, the adult male moved in. This time I could really feel his anger myself, his refusal to "go to the light", was spat at me - with venom.
He was laughing and deriding our efforts, he was feeling very powerful.
Tracy was very uncomfortable and began to shake and writhe in her seat.
I tightened my grip on Tracy's hand as I realised that the energy coming up through my feet was flowing through me and out into Tracy.
I heard Jon say, "what can we do?"
I heard a reply from Armon which was, *"you must ask, that he go with love and understanding"*.
I repeated this to the circle and we all silently asked for the "love and understanding".

Speaking for myself; I began to ask for "love and understanding", through clenched teeth.
It is a logical and simple thing to ask for - in the cold light of day – when your adrenaline isn't flowing. But,

having felt the energy of this man, and the strength of his spite, and, witnessed the struggle and fear of the children, replayed, through the actions of Tracy - it is not as simple a request as it first appears.

I felt the man leave.
Armon told me that the man was now back in the Spirit world.

This had been an amazing first time Spirit release experience.
One I would not forget and one that I would learn from.

Then, as now, I understand, that for me to do this work
– the protection and guidance of my guides, an open –
non-judgmental mind, and clear and precise
communication is the key to a successful and peaceful
Spirit release.

It was also around this time that I was instructed in the art of training my spirit to leave my body and return to it - safely.

Armon guided me through this procedure as I lay flat on my back.
With his guidance and my subsequent practice - I learned how to allow my spirit to leave my body – noting that it was joined to my physical body by means of a chord (my re-entry point) and after a short time, re entering my body, followed by re-aligning my energy centres.

I was quickly instructed to develop and use this technique for remote earth and house clearance and eventually, for Spirit release. Indeed by February 1994 I was clearing a negative energy line (which had been pointed out to me by a dowser whom John had met whilst on a dowsing course) from our own home and from the house next door.

Armon guided me through this daily procedure, beginning on 13th February and ending on the 8th of March 1994.

Although I have the log of my findings which is a list of lines checked and corresponding decreasing numbers (as the work was undertaken), I have decided that it to include it would serve no useful purpose. Suffice it to say that I was hearing and seeing the relevant numbers and using A/C for confirmation.
Looking through my notebooks, whilst writing this book, I spotted this entry:

Whilst sleeping, during the night of 3rd/4th February 1994. I kept hearing the phrase;
"You'll be Dowsing Dowsing Dowsing......Everything!"

Someone is irritated!

CHAPTER EIGHT

WILLIAM.

I was listening to music – this time Rossini's "William Tell Overture". I didn't realise how animated and excited I was becoming. As the music played and played, louder and louder, I became quite exhausted from jigging around the room – the phrases "Off her head" and "As high as a kite" come to mind as I plonked, exhausted, down in my chair.
I was buzzing from head to toe.
As I sat in my chair I became aware that someone in Spirit had their hands on my feet – I was being grounded – down and down – re-connecting with the earth, my breathing beginning to return to normal, coming back down off the ceiling.

I was fortunate that someone was watching over me – again. I was very grateful that "they" were looking after me, because I know it would have taken me time to realise just what I needed to do to bring me "down to earth" and what's more – I was feeling sick!

I was in a mood full of self-assurance that night, as I set off with John to Tracy and Jon's for an evening, where a group of people had been invited "to meet our guides" if we wanted to.

Of course I knew that Mum, Dad and Armon were my guides and Tracy had explained that Mum's dad was a Doorkeeper (a protector) but it would be nice to speak to them again - if they came.

We were instructed to sit in a circle and we were each given a piece of paper and a pen.
Sitting with our eyes closed we were told to ask who our guide was.
Quick as a flash I heard.

"William"

As both my Granddads had been christened William I thought it must be one of them but the energy in front of me felt very strong and slightly threatening.

Next question: "Why are you here?"

"Communication"

I began to feel a little uneasy in this presence – Granddad must be cross I thought.

Next question: "Why have you come to do this work?"

"Because I am good at it!" the answer snapped back.

I knew now that I didn't recognise this presence, this was not one of my Granddads'.
This William sounded very abrupt and bossy, unfriendly, strict and what's more, I realised - he had come for me!
I had a feeling of foreboding.

Tracy on the other hand, seemed to be very pleased for me. "Well you've met your guide," she said smiling.

"Yes – great" I replied with more than a little apprehension.

All my efforts in raising vibrations had, until now, been a means for me to speak to my family. Now, the realisation dawned, that more was expected of me, that somehow, in my willingness to learn to communicate more clearly I had indicated a desire to communicate with strangers!

I had stepped onto this path of discovery without realising it.

I had had, a wish to play the piano but not the will to learn.
Now, I had the wish to communicate AND had indicated that I had a will to learn – apparently!

During that brief meeting – my initial impression of William was that he had a very high opinion of himself and his ability to teach - my instant reaction was "well if he thinks he's going to boss me around – he can think again!"

Lying in bed that same night, I was suddenly aware that a man in a dark suit was standing very close to my side of the bed – just standing staring at me – saying nothing.
I dived under the bed covers and said the only thing that I knew to say – "Go to the light – Go to the light". I lay and listened. Hearing nothing – I peeped out from under the covers to see if he had gone.
No – he was still there.
I dived again – "Go to the light, Go to the light" I implored.
Once more I peered out from my refuge – he was still there! – still standing, still saying nothing.

As I lay and squinted at him with one eye (the other eye was still under the covers) I realised that "he" was this "new" William.

Realising that he had no intention of moving, and not knowing what to say next, I merely said, "Goodnight" and turned over very quickly onto my side pulling the bedding over my head as I went.

Emerging from under the bed covers the next morning, I was relieved to find that "he" had gone.

"Maybe he had moved on, perhaps he had just come to Tracy and Jons' to visit – just passing through sort of thing?"

Wrong.

Later that morning William came again.

I asked the same three questions that I had asked the previous night, and I received the same three answers in exactly the same manner.

He obviously wasn't a chatty sort of Spirit, which left me feeling at a loss as to what I could ask or do next and so I did the obvious thing – nothing.

However, the next morning when he came again (still in the smart suit) he said.

"You will drive to the house where you grew up and park your car by a stick that you will see lying in the gutter.

You will walk down the path and into the field.

You will speak to someone.

You will walk back to your car and you will see Mr Trelfa.

You will come back home".

It was at this point that John came into the room and said "What are you doing today?"

"Well it seems that I'm going out" I replied, telling him what William had said.

The thought that I could just ignore William and his instructions never entered my head.
As far as I saw things, I had nothing to lose by going for a walk in the field that was behind the house where I had grown up – I had done it many times before.

So it was with some scepticism and amusement, mixed with a tinge of "Who does he think he is – playing stupid games" that I set off on my journey.

To clarify things I will remind you that the house referred to is the house into which I moved at the age of 6yrs – the ex rectory by the churchyard.
The house where I lived with Mum, Dad and my sister, not forgetting to mention the four dogs.
The place where our neighbours were Mr and Mrs Trelfa and their children, and Susan (noted for her upside down pineapple cake)
The house into which John moved. Where we lived with my parents for the first 2 years of our marriage.
A place that I had known for 17 years.

The street hadn't changed since I had last visited and as I slowed the car down to park I noticed that the house was for sale again, and then I saw the stick.

Just as William had said – there lying in the gutter was a stick which is about 18 inches long and approximately 1 inch in diameter (I say, "is" because you won't be surprised to know that I still have it).

Having parked the car and with the stick in my hand, I set off down the narrow path which runs along the side of the garden and the church.

Reaching the wooden stile (still intact) I "stepped back in time" remembering how, when I was a child, one of our dogs – Shep – would come to the field with me and we would wander around looking for rabbit holes (not to chase rabbits you understand – Shep just "sniffed").

I also had the memory of Dad chasing after Shep as the dog went in pursuit of any bitch in season who happened to live within a 2-mile radius.

As I stood now, and looked down into the field, I remembered how the long grass parted, showing the route that the dog was taking, I could see the flashes of black furry tail which would tantalisingly reveal his progress through the grass.

Dad in hot pursuit shouting the dog to "heel" as he ran.

The funny thing was that most of these bitches seemed to live across two fields, over the dual carriageway, and deep into the depths of a housing estate, a foot journey that could take anything up to one and a half-hours!

I grinned as I remembered their return; the sight of the slobber and the redness of the dogs' tongue as it lolled out of the side of his face, and the redness and sweat that poured off Dad's face - both of them panting.

No one daring to speak to Dad!

It was very hard not to laugh on these occasions and unfortunately, I never tried hard enough – earning myself - one of dad's famous scowls, ("the look") designed to put you in your place - but only resulting in making me titter all the more.

Thankfully, we dog owners are generally much more responsible these days.
"The operation" being a very common–place solution to a variety of "doggy" problems, as our last dog Jack discovered, before John and I moved to North Wales.
I have several characteristics of my Dad, one being - ironically, my sense of humour.
But there was no way that I was going to be the one who hopelessly ran after a wanton dog!

But back to the story:

I climbed over the stile and walked a little way into the field - alongside the church wall.
Leaning against the wall, I wondered what to do next, and whilst I was thinking, I began to strip the bark off the stick.
Just as I was thinking of walking further into the field – I heard a noise to my left.
Looking towards the stile, I saw a lady climbing over it into the field, and, remembering Williams' prediction, I said "Hello" as she passed me.
The woman smiled, said "hello" and continued walking.

Watching her walk away, I said to William
"What now?"

"*You can have all this*" came back the reply.

"What do you mean – the field – the house?"

There was no answer.

Did he mean John and I could buy the house? He obviously didn't know that our new business wasn't going very well.

This thought brought me back to everyday matters and so I decided to return to the car.
As I walked back down the path, I peered through the hedge into my "old" garden. A few changes had been made to the design of the garden, but basically, it still looked the same.

On reaching the footpath, I was thrilled to see Mr Trelfa standing by his gate – just as William had said.
"Hello" he shouted as he noticed me "What are you doing here?"

"Oh I just thought I would come and walk down the field" I replied.

We chatted about the house being for sale and caught up on how everyone was - it was great to see him again after a gap of about 12 years.

Driving home, I thought how brilliant it had all been. Everything had happened exactly as William had said it would - amazing!
The stick was incredible, did William just see it there and hope it was still lying on the ground when I arrived? or did he put it there?. Anyway – it didn't matter did it? Everything was as William said it would be and William now, had my full attention - and my respect.

At the same time as I was beginning to communicate with William and becoming used to his daily presence,

John was swiftly developing his healing and dowsing skills.

One day, John was asked to visit a friend's house to dowse for any problems that may have been affecting the family.

Keen to practice my dowsing skills with my apple core, we decided to go together.

The morning of the visit arrived and I woke to discover that I had developed a cold virus overnight. I felt awful, streaming nose and eyes, generally feeling unwell. I was not happy - in fact I was really fed up. This was my first opportunity to dowse for someone – to show off my skill – I really didn't feel very well - it was obvious to me, that I would have to stay at home.

John left me lying on the settee clutching a box of tissues – sulking.

"Go and have a bath". said William.

"What – Oh leave me alone". I muttered.

"Go and have a bath" repeated William – a little louder.

"I don't want a bath – why would I want to have a bath now". I couldn't understand why William couldn't just leave me alone to wallow in my misery.

"Go and Have A Bath!" he ordered.

I had had enough of this conversation – "Oh for goodness sake – alright – I'll go and have a bath".
Maybe a bath would make me feel better I thought as I climbed the stairs en route to the bathroom.

Returning to the settee after my bath, I thankfully lay down and closed my eyes.

I began to see a garden with a path and trees and at the same time I realised that I was lying with my hands together – fingers touching – palms' apart – forming a pointed arch.

"Why am I doing this – William?" I asked, nodding towards my hands.

"That's the well" came back the reply.

I realised that I was in the same garden that John was in and being shown where the problems areas were. I immediately I jumped up – cold forgotten - and found a piece of paper and a pen and began to draw what I was being shown.

When John came home he told me of all the things that he had found and as I listened to his descriptions, I knew that I had been told some of the same things.
Confidently, I stood up and passed him my sketch – I couldn't help grinning smugly as he looked at it.

"You've drawn the garden - and the well is exactly where you've shown it".

To say that I was pleased, would have been putting it mildly - and John seemed to be impressed as well.

I was going to enjoy working with William and of course, my Granddad William who was my protector, my gatekeeper.
I remember talking to John about my fear of getting the two of them mixed up; "after all" I reasoned, "I can't

just say to you – William is here – you won't know just which William it is – will you?"

I remember concentrating very hard, when tuning in to their unique vibrations - to ensure that I knew exactly which of the two Williams' were there.

This was a very good opportunity for me to practice the recognition of particular Spirit energy; it encouraged me to be more sensitive to my own vibrations' and to those of Spirit energy.

I was working to refine them all the time.

William sometimes joked with me in those early days: - *"Hello, it's just me – just William"*

William let me know, on a regular basis, that he was aware of every conversation that I had. That he saw everything that I saw. I had no hiding place – not that I wanted one now. Being a bossy person myself, I used to jokingly moan about my lack of privacy, "Is nothing sacred!" was my usual outburst – challenging William to answer me back.

The cold cleared up quickly and I realised, on reflection, what a blessing it had been. Because of it, I had been given the opportunity to experience working remotely with William, and that had been a wonderful experience. I also realised that William, who had come to teach me communication – didn't want me to dowse. Furthermore, it had been William who had said, in that dream *"You'll be dowsing, dowsing, dowsing"* - and as for my apple core – well it went back into the drawer.

There would be no more dowsing with a pendulum, for me. In fact on those occasional times, when I did reach for A/C again – those immortal words would come back to haunt me;

"You'll be dowsing, dowsing, dowsing", and I would quickly put my A/C back in the drawer.

The issue of the cold was also interesting to me and I began to wonder if it had been chosen deliberately, as some sort of weird joke.

By saying that I must explain myself. As a child and before the age of 6yrs, I had the ability to "develop" a cold at will – particularly during a Sunday afternoon – in the hope that I could avoid the final visit of the day to church.

The onset of my sudden cold was very convincing - I thought.

I would sniff and blow my way through many hankies throughout the afternoon – taking each used hankie as evidence, to show Mum.

All my efforts were rewarded (occasionally) by Mum and I missing the evening service.

I suspect that mum saw straight through my ruse – she wasn't a person who could be easily duped – but nonetheless, she would sometimes allow me to win the battle of wills. Dad's remedy for my "colds" was to make a picture book for me. The book contained coloured pictures - dog, horse, chicken and duck - are the ones that I remember; and I would sit, during those long sermons, looking through the my book.

So, I wondered, "had the tables had been turned on me?" – if they had; if this had been some Karmic punishment - it served me right. It would also indicate that William might, after all, have a sense of humour.

As John and I were lying in bed one night, he being asleep but with one hand on my leg, I felt a sudden and strong, electric shock coming from John's hand into my leg. I shot out of bed like a stone released from a catapult, my heart thumping. John, to my amazement, lay undisturbed and oblivious, and so I went down stairs to ask William what had happened.

He explained that John's healing energy was getting stronger and simply – I had felt a discharge of that energy.

So it was that it was with some trepidation that I took up John's offer of healing, for the first time.

I had two complaints, one being a lump in the groin (a non operational hernia) the pain from which ran up my stomach and was only relieved by my crouching, and holding my stomach until the pain ceased, an action that could be embarrassing if I was walking in the street at the time. Not as embarrassing as the actual diagnosis of course, when a group of medical students were brought in to the consultation room to each assess the severity of my lump, and I was repeatedly asked to cough for each and every one of them.

My second ailment was a torn ligament and a torn muscle on either side of my right knee.

Although I had had treatment for these injuries I still suffered pain and my knee would lock. The only way to unlock it was to hold the top of my knee and swing my leg until it unlocked.

For those of you out there who have a wicked sense of humour like myself; I hope you are enjoying yourselves now; as the picture emerges of me in the supermarket – clutching my groin with my left hand, whilst standing on one leg – clutching my right knee with my right hand, and swinging my leg to and fro.

Oh, and I forgot to mention that I had developed a habit of singing to myself as I did it.

During that first healing session I felt a tingling sensation around my knee and a fizzing sensation inside my knee and at first, when John began the healing on my groin, I felt the same thing, It was only immediately afterward, that the pain began. I was in agony from my groin. "What have you done – it's worse – Oh it really hurts". I was bending over clutching my stomach.
"Just wait a few minutes," said an unruffled John.

The pain did subside and within half an hour the lump had noticeably shrunk. I was amazed and kept having to check it's status. "I think it's gone down again" I would report.
John did give me some more healing and the lump in my groin shrank to nothing, the pain disappeared.
I very occasionally feel a twinge from the area but that is all.
As for my knee, it was quickly healed; enabling me to sit crossed legged on the floor for hours without pain – my favourite position when listening to music.

I was now "sitting" everyday, grounding myself and practising raising my vibrations and of course listening to music.
My inner vibrations were quickening and my senses, particularly hearing and seeing, were becoming keener.
I began to feel an inner buzzing sensation when Spirit were around, particularly around and above my head.
This activity around my head was intense, and usually indicated that William was near. As if to confirm this, in answer to my question "Is that you William?" he began to interfere with my train of thought and would on many occasions – render me speechless – a practice that I found very irritating to say the least.
There I would be in the middle of a conversation - and suddenly I couldn't remember what I was going to say

next. For someone like me who has an opinion on most things - and a will to express it – I found this interference extremely annoying.

"Oh for goodness sake, William!" was one of my politest exclamations.

I felt very much that William was wanting to control me, as of course he did, but not in any sinister way.

Once I had learned to accept and laugh at my plight instead of losing my temper, I realised that I was responding to these events, by asking William a question.

To coin a phrase "the penny had dropped".

I came to understand that - "when I feel this energy descend on me, I must STOP and ask WHY or WHAT?"

It became obvious to me that this technique was being used to indicate that it was time to, for example: "close down" my chakras? – that maybe I should ask for protection? – at least, I must stop and ask William why he was doing this.

I was beginning to understand that I must learn something from everything that William said or did, however obscure the "everything" was - it all happened for a reason – it was all for my benefit.

I also knew that I loved William and he loved me.

When I had been in the presence of Spirit in previous times, I had felt the love that they had for me. It is a love that oozes from their very being, a love which penetrates, a love which can be overwhelming.

William oozed this same love – unconditional, inspirational and for – ever.

William was with me all the time, in the house; whilst cutting the grass, in the supermarket queue (which he found very boring) and whilst I was driving. I well remember the first time I heard him call my name as I was driving down a country lane; I immediately slowed the car down – just in time to avoid a speeding car coming the opposite direction and on my side of the road.

Other guides since, have given me prior warnings, particularly when I am driving but I have yet to receive a warning of a police speed trap – some things - I just have to take the responsibility for myself!

It was now early April 1994 and John was seeing patients for healing sessions.

Williams' communication was invaluable to both myself and John and I had begun to write it all down in a notebook. Obviously I cannot relate any communication with relevance to John's patients – but here are a couple of communications, relevant to myself.

7th April 1994, Armon .

"Hi ya kid, how are you doing? – just popped in for a progress report. William will tell me how you are doing, but I'm watching"

"Send positive energy out for yourself, as you do for other people and the lines. The positive energy will be received by other people and sent back to you – this is helpful, both for business and your spiritual path"

"Buy more note pads"

William:

"You are working with me – and we have a plan, as you develop, we go down our path.
I am in charge, but I will bend and will look at different things, but you have many important steps to take – we will do them together at your pace.
You will learn patience and diplomacy like you have never dreamt of.
But Oh what a lot of work to do yet!"

"Learn your lessons and learn them well and they will stay with you to be used to the best of your ability – which is all anyone could ask of you"

I was full of hope and expectation for an exciting future, working and learning with William and Armon.
John was also really enjoying all the things he was discovering and putting into practice.
We were still going to see Tracy and Jon and all these things together, allowed us to put aside the ongoing financial worries that we had.

.

.

CHAPTER NINE

AN EXPERIENCE.

Whenever John and I went to visit Tracy and Jon, Williams' energy would become particularly strong and oppressive. His energy would descend on me and I knew that he didn't want me to participate in any more group activity, leaving me no option but to sit aside from the group – usually on the floor, in the corner of the room.

When I asked William why he was doing this, he said:

"You are stopped because it makes it more difficult for you to fit in – so you have to make a special effort to join in – you could have walked away, it would have been easy".

"You know it links us stronger, because you trust me and you are accepted by the group, for just behaving the way you do".

When I asked William to repeat his reply, just in case I had missed something, he said:

"Must I repeat everything!"

"You are working with ME and WE have a plan as you develop on your path".

"I am in charge, but I will bend, and will look at different things, but you have many important steps to take".

"Tracy and Jon give you understanding".

"You will learn patience and diplomacy – like you have never dreamt of".

"Now about this puppy!"

This last line referred to conversations' John and I were having, about the possibility of having another dog sometime in the future.

Tracy and Jon introduced us to a male friend of theirs' who I will refer to as "P", for the purpose of this narration.

"P" had moved in with them – he introduced himself as a Hypnotherapist, a Tarot reader, and a person who also who had an interest in crystals.

My first impressions of "P" was that he was a quiet man who didn't say very much.
He was very often in his room when we arrived and therefore we didn't see very much of him at all.
It had been arranged that one evening "P" would lead the group of us that met at Tracy and Jon's in a meditation evening and I was very pleased that William (for once) seemed to have no objection to my participation.
I did not write any notes on this event, nor do I remember any details now – I was just happy to have been able to join in.

Increasingly there would be an atmosphere at Tracy and Jon's house, a sort of heavy feeling as if there had been an argument, I began to get the feeling that perhaps Tracy was getting fed – up of having a visitor – he had now been staying for a few weeks.

One evening as we arrived, the atmosphere was very heavy.

Needing the bathroom, I went towards the stairs and as I lifted my foot to tread on the bottom stair – I heard a rattle snake shake it's tail. This "snake" was sitting on the bottom step.

I stepped over it and went to the bathroom, here the atmosphere was really heavy and I had the feeling that I was being "told" to go away.

I instinctively knew that all this was being caused by "P" and arriving back downstairs, I told Tracy about the "snake" and asked Tracy, in whispered tones, where he was

She told me that he was in his room and that he had been in there all afternoon.

On another occasion, "P" brought his Tarot cards out and he invited me to pick three cards.

I had never had anything to do with Tarot cards before and didn't know how they worked and to be honest with you, I had no interest in them, but I picked three cards out anyway, hoping that that would be the end of the matter.

"P" got very excited when he looked at the cards and kept saying "I've never seen this before – never all three together".

He didn't seem able to explain what he meant, and as I wasn't interested to know, the subject was changed, but I noticed that "P" spent the rest of the evening in what can only be described as a sullen silence, until he returned to his room.

It was two or three days after this incident, that John and I received a telephone call from Jon, to say that he and Tracy wanted to come and see us both.

On their arrival, and with the obligatory mug of tea in hand, Jon produced a selection of crystals and a piece of paper with a hand – drawn diagram on it. The crystals were a selection of rough quartz, and if my memory serves me correctly, there were five of them.

These crystals, we were told, were a present from them, and, placed as directed on the diagram, under our bed, they would help to cleanse the house - by clearing any negativity, and the crystals would also improve our financial situation.

We had no hesitation in placing the crystals under our bed that night.

We had only been in bed about ten or fifteen minutes, when suddenly I heard, from another bedroom, the sound of a foot being stamped in the floor, along with the sound of "P"s voice saying in a laughing tone – "I'm here".

At the same moment, John sat up and said – "The bed's shaking – get out of it",
Both of us jumped out of bed and as I stood shaking, John said – "The crystals". With that he dived under the bed. collected the crystals together, ran down the stairs, unlocked the back door, and threw the crystals outside.

I followed in his wake, heart pounding and still shaking.

"What's happened? Has there been an earthquake? "P"s here, What are you doing with the crystals?"

I was so confused.
I told John that I had heard "P" stamp his foot and shout.

John replied – "I didn't hear that, but I knew as soon as I felt the bed shaking that he had programmed the crystals to give him remote access to our home - that was why the bed was shaking".

John was angry and I was too shaken to be angry. I was scared.
"P" had sounded so menacing and I could still feel his energy.
Sleep was beyond me that night.

The next day I rang Tracy to tell her what had happened and I felt that her repeated explanation about the crystals being there to help us, only meant that she hadn't grasped how horrible the experience had been. And I felt that she thought that I must be mistaken when I said that "P" had visited us.

That night as we went to bed, I tried not to think about the previous nights' activity but it was with some horror, that once again, I heard the stamp of the foot, and those words "I'm here".

I nudged John and said - "P"s back".
We both lay there, feeling his nasty presence.
Sleep eluded us both.
I didn't hear "P" say anything else, but his mere presence was threatening.

The days and nights with this continuous onslaught, turned into weeks.

During the day I would try not to think about "P" because every time I did, I would feel his presence.

I was unable to communicate with William or anyone else, having being told by William in that first day or two, that I must "close down" all my chakras until this attack was over. My understanding was that, if I attempted to open my chakras, I was opening up to any Spirit who was around, thus allowing "P" to move in.

This is a piece of advice that I have never forgotten - a lesson well learnt:

A piece of advice that I have passed to other people who have found themselves in a similar situation.

Aside from John, I felt totally isolated.

We did have another conversation with Tracy and Jon, during which they revealed that the crystals were actually a "gift" from "P". He had suggested to them, that it would be better if John and I weren't told that they had come from him and so Tracy and Jon had gone along with his suggestion.

During that conversation, John warned Jon to make sure that his (Jon's) thoughts' were not being interfered with, or influenced by, "P".

The intensity of these menacing attacks increased, which resulted in my inability to sleep.

On hearing "P"s arrival, I would get out of bed and go and sit in the living room, only to have "P" standing in front of me telling me to go to bed. Sometimes he would shout from upstairs – "Come back to bed!"

"You should be in bed now".

He even tried to make me believe that it was my mother who was ordering me, or John.

He actually attempted to imitate their voices.

Whenever I did try to fall asleep, he would come. He would always announce his arrival by stamping on the floor and saying, "I'm here", then I would feel his energy moving across the landing and into our room. At first he would stand by the bed, looking at me, oozing pleasure at my obvious fear but, as time went on, he began to attempt to lie on top of me, repeating the words – "You know you want me to – never mind about John – you know you want me to".
I would struggle with him in order to get out from underneath him.

Night after night.

I was now too scared to close my eyes, and so in order to help me, John, who was also aware of "P"s presence, would stay awake - on watch, which gave me the confidence to snatch some sleep.

We did contact Tracy and Jon again, to tell them that we wouldn't be going to see them whilst "P" was there and I passed the information that I had been given by William just before I had closed down, which was that "P" will sacrifice his life - and that is, alright " in other words – he would commit suicide.

I knew that the more I thought about "P", and the nasty way he was behaving, the more power over me he would have. I knew, and John had advised me, that I mustn't think about him. But knowing that and putting that knowledge into practice, when my thoughts were driven by fear, confusion and anger was not an easy task.

But it is possible to do – with effort and determination.

John and I never knew why "P" embarked on this attack, an attack which lasted the best part of three months – neither do we know why he stopped.

There was a part of me who blamed spirit for allowing this to happen to me.
I didn't understand why they didn't stop him.
It was only after the event, and after William's return, that I could begin to see the positive aspects, which were:-

By not "opening up", I believe that I shortened the length of time that this attack went on for.

It taught me to take more responsibility for my own protection (I wouldn't forget to ask for protection again), and made me more aware of the importance of a Gatekeeper.

I refrained from attempting to retaliate. (a big temptation for me – futile though it may have been).

I survived unharmed.

Out of the blue, in January 1995, John and I came home to find a message on our answer - phone. It was from Jon (we hadn't seen or heard from them for months).
He rang to say that "P" had committed suicide.

CHAPTER TEN

MORE FRIENDS THAN YOU KNOW.

The weeks of April, May and early June 1994 were a horrible time.
The attack by "P" was bad enough, but the loss of contact with William and everyone else left me feeling very lonely, confused, and with many unanswered questions.
My life had been full of excitement, joy, communication and love at the beginning of the year, and now I felt that all these things had been taken away from me.

One day at the end of May/early June, I was sitting, listening to music.
I felt so miserable and sorry for myself - I was crying and calling out loud, "William, William" – calling for him to come.

It was through the noise of my crying that I heard: -

"Hello"

I immediately stopped crying and said a startled "hello" back, my heart pounding.

"Hello – I thought I would come to speak to you".

I could feel the love and concern of this Spirit flowing into me, I felt safe within the energy of him, which made me cry again – this time the tears were tears of gratitude and relief.

"Oh thank–you for coming – thank–you" I was so excited.
"Who are you?"

He told me his name was Rangu and said that he was Mongolian.
Then, referring to the music that was playing he said: -

"This reminds me of the forest.
Nature makes music.
Some people have listened to nature and have made instruments - to copy it – so that they can hear the wind in the trees, whenever they want it, or need it.
A rock can make music, remember your dream – the vibrations – you have heard it".

N.B. Dream referred to in Ch 6.

I was amazed that he knew about my dream.

A light was beginning to dawn within me – a light that indicated that everyone, both in this physical world, and within the Spirit world, were linked together.

A light that indicated that whatever happened in my life (or any-ones life) was witnessed by a host of Spirits, and those Spirits did not have to be known to us personally.
I was thrilled and grateful that he had come and I was so glad that I could still hear and speak to Spirit.

This brings me back to the subject of note taking. I must explain that, sometimes I would receive the communication and then write in the notebook afterwards, but, increasingly – the notes were taken by John as I passed the communication on.

Looking back through my notes (to help in the writing of this book) I am absolutely staggered and dismayed, to discover that I hadn't dated the exact time when William returned.

But return he did. Oh happy day!

He was, and still is, a huge influence in my life and certainly in my development as a medium, I can hear him tutting now, as I own up to my lack of discipline in the early days of my note taking.

The communication began again. My constant companion was back.

Putting the past few weeks behind me, I was eager to pick – up my communication with William and others as quickly as possible and William was just as eager, and so I began to "sit" every night in order to receive their communication.

William always came through first and then would step aside for others to pass their communication, usually in response to the many questions John and I had.
Seeing William first, before sensing another presence, always gave me the reassurance and freedom I needed to raise my vibrations and focus on that new energy.
I felt safe, and trusted that if William stood aside to allow the spirit to stand in front of me, then it was safe for me to continue.

I will share a fraction of that communication with you now.

WILLIAM. To me:

"Be thankful for the night and glad for the day – whatever it may bring".

"Don't misuse the gift – respect it and know it for what it is.
Keep your feet on the floor – and NEVER forget – it can be taken away.
And if it is taken away from you – you will have let me down".

"I'm not supposed to say that – but we understand one another".

WILLIAM. To John.

"A healers work is never done, but you can't heal everybody you come across".

Qu: What can you tell me about Bach Flower Remedies?

Ans:
"It is a different subject on it's own.
It would need serious study,
There would be no harm in finding out more information, but it would need time to study.
Have you got the time?"

Qu: Is it necessary to have a picture of someone, when asking for healing.
"We are all linked – we are universal.
A picture would focus your mind.
We do not need to look at a picture".

John's guide, Kuru, began to use me to pass information to John and would also come to answer his questions.

When John asked her for guidance on a particular aspect of healing, she was very precise in her answers.

In respect of one new patient in particular, who was seriously ill with cancer, she told him exactly how many times that patient should be seen in the first week, and then the second week, and so on.

It was Kuru who suggested to both of us that, regarding the question of, "How often to ask for distant healing?" – we must allow time for the healing to do it's work and therefore, to ask every night for the same person, was un–necessary, and unhelpful. She suggested that we ask every third night.

One evening Kuru and Megan (my Spirit sister) came. Megan had previously told me that she "greeted" people when they "pass over".

In response to my question to Megan "What happens when people "pass over" into the Spirit world, Megan replied: -

"When people arrive, they need time and healing. They don't just jump up.
It is very rewarding work
The delight on their faces when they see their loved ones, is something that never fails to touch the heart.
There are those who arrive and don't need healing and counselling because they have known that they will carry on in this better place.
They are left to spend as much time with their family and friends – until they want to contribute.
Some are just happy to "BE".
Others are ready to contribute or work, as you call it – but there is no time limit".

"I was told by a counsellor, on many occasions, that my parents would eventually arrive and I was eager to see them – even though I grew up apart from them – we are still linked – still family – until such times as one of us chooses another family, or the same family, but at a much later time".

Qu. to Kuru
"If Megan chose to be born into another family, how could she still be linked to Mum and Dad?"

Ans: *"She would still exist as Megan".*

I found it really strange to hear Megan speak about her parents going to see her and know that she was speaking about the deaths of my parents.
How happy she must have been – how sad I had been.

On another evening, John's mum (Elsie) popped in. I always love to see Elsie and this particular evening she had brought someone with her. The conversation went as follows: -

Elsie:
"Fancy letting Lynn paint that ceiling" (A reference to my decorating the living room)
"I've brought somebody with me to say hello".

Me:
"There's a man"

"Hi son".

Me: (I could see him now).
"It's your Granddad – your Mum's dad".

John:
"Hi Granddad".

Elsie:
"He's been pestering me to come and now he's not saying anything".

Granddad:
"How are Everton doing?" (Reference to the Football Club)

John: laughing.
"I like the mints" (a reference to the fact that Everton Football Club are nicknamed "the toffees")

"What have you been doing Mum?"

Elsie:
"Spending time with trees,
Been learning about trees and plants and Atmosphere –
all very scientific.
Very interested in science.
Learning things I didn't have chance to learn before.
It's like being at school".

On another occasion, John and I were introduced to a child whom William brought with him.
She introduced herself as Laura and said that she was eight.
William said that Laura had wanted to come and say "Hello" earlier, during the evenings' communication, but that he had made her wait. He described her as an impatient, pesky child.

We were to meet Laura on many more occasions.

In response to the question John and I asked William: "Have you any comment to make about the way the World is now?" He replied:

"Nations are learning to live together but it is very fragile.
The thread between the nations is weak and it will not be governments that strengthen the threads – but the people.
A mass journey together, of the peoples all over the World.
The power is with the people, not the governments.
And it is only the people who will change the World
The governments are driven by power alone.
People are driven by existence – from the basic need to eat – to wanting a comfortable life for themselves.
The power is the peoples.
The people from all corners of the World.

There will be an economic drive to join hands across the World, and this joining of hands will come about – due to government's mis–handling of finances.

People and businesses will muster together and take charge of their own lives.
Through this action – an understanding of peoples' customs and ways of life, will join nations together.
People must learn to understand the needs of others and this is why it is people and people alone, who ensure the survival of the planet.

Here endeth this morning's lesson".

It was during these weeks, that a friend and work associate of ours, suddenly collapsed and died, having suffered a heart attack.

"A" had worked as a graphic artist. One evening it was a great surprise to both John and I when, as William stepped aside – "A" appeared.
He spoke to John: -

"Hi mate.
Well this is a "turn – up".
You ought to see the paintings here – I was going to say they're out of this world – if you know what I mean.
The colours here are amazing.
I'm on top of the world – that's a joke".

"A" then went on to ask John to go and see his wife and children, as he had some concerns about them and he asked that John visit on a particular day – at a particular time, which John agreed to.

John returned from that visit on the Sunday morning, as arranged -and it was obvious that he wasn't feeling very well.
He looked pale and said that he was tired and so he went to lie down.
A few minutes later, I went upstairs to see him, only to find that he could hardly speak - he was finding it hard to breath and appeared to be sinking into unconsciousness.
This was all happening so quickly.
I knew we needed help and the person who came to mind was Stan, the dowser we had met.
Thankfully, Stan answered the telephone when I rang, and I quickly told him what was happening.

"I'll come straight away," he said.

It seemed to take a long time for Stan to arrive, (only about 15 or 20 minutes actually) and all the time we were waiting, John was drifting further away.

In my panic, I asked for some healing energy for him myself – holding my hand over him as I asked, I had never asked before, neither did I feel any energy, but it was the only thing I could do.

It was great relief that I opened the door to Stan.

Stan immediately went into the bedroom.

John was hardly able to acknowledge Stans' presence - not being able to breath properly, speak, or focus his eyes.

Gradually, as Stan's pendulum swung first one way and then another (in answer to his questions), John began to re-gain consciousness.

It was a very slow process.

When Stan was happy that John was on the way to recovery, he and I left John to rest and we went downstairs for a much-needed cup of tea. Stan explained how "A" had moved into John's energy field, so much so that John was feeling those last moments of "A"s life, as it ebbed away.

About fifteen minutes later John came down to join us. His colour had improved but he was still having some difficulty in breathing, and he spoke in a weakened voice. But it was a great relief to see him standing, all be it wobbly, and to see him smile wryly, shaking his head in amazement – as he realised exactly what had happened to him.

One the advice of Stan, he returned to bed in order to recover fully – which he did.

This was another experience that was sudden and shocking in nature – we needed more explanation and information on how to avoid this happening again in the future: -

19th June 1994. Extract from notebook.

William has explained that John's metabolism was increased and then decreased when "A" moved into his energy field.
John's body didn't know where its natural level was – which had the effect of sending John into shock.
"A" was sorry for what had happened.
William says that "A" is not "stuck" (earthbound), and that in passing his symptoms onto John – "A" had freed himself from the earthplane.

William told us that neither John nor I recognised the symptoms early enough, and our delay in getting help, meant *"things got a little out of hand"*.
He added that John could have *"ticked over at that slow pace for 2 – 3 hours"*.
He assured us that no physical damage had been done.

Qu: There must be a practical use for this "ticking over?"

Ans: *"Levitation"*

William then suggested that it would be a good idea for John to have a healing session with Stan, to *"centre and balance him"* - John said that he would arrange it.

It was during this session with William, that I felt another strong energy descending on me.
As the energy descended, I attempted to travel "up–wards" through it, in an attempt to "tune in", whilst I

was doing this – I had the impression in my mind's eye of a female American Indian.

At the same time, I felt another energy – this time it was young Laura:

"Don't ignore me," she said.

I got confused with these different energies and I heard William say:

"Close down".

I closed down.

The next evening William said: -

"You let your mind get in the way – which caused your confusion".

He went on to explain that; as an open channel, I could unwittingly invite other spirits to come, these spirits could be difficult for a spirit guide to control.

He reminded me that I was to work on a "one to one" basis with him; that I must ground myself and ask for white light. He added: -

"I don't mind a queue, as long as it is my queue".

At this point the vibrational gap between William and I became much less and instead of passing communication to me – he passed communication through me: -

"In my opinion you should pay more attention to grounding yourself – when you feel the need –
But I would go further than that and say it should become routine – everyday – and after a healing session,
We don't want a chink in the armour".

"I want to be able to control the Spirit guided to Lynn, because she will be a target in the future – a bright light.. Unfortunately, this brings hazards".

From my perspective, I found it a strange experience to pass communication about myself – using my name. It was the fact that William was having this conversation with John – as though I wasn't there – yet I could hear what was being said – it felt weird!

On another evening, whilst channelling William, I detected another spirit energy.
William asked:

"What are you going to do now?"

Remembering the last occasion when this had happened I asked for white light and also asked William to identify the Spirit.

"Good girl ----- Chinook".

As William said the name, I was aware of an Indian Brave, who, as William told me; *"hadn't come to speak – just to look".*
As I looked at William, I sensed that there was something else for me to do, I looked from one to another, hoping for the right answer to come to me. Looking at the Brave and with Williams' statement that the Brave had only come to look – I asked the Brave to leave – and he did.

No comment was made, nor did I ask if I had done the correct thing – only time and William would tell.
I noted in my book, after the event, that this felt like an exercise – a test.

This communication business was getting complicated – there was obviously a lot for me to learn.

I was really enjoying all the communication – the visits' from William, Kuru, Armon, Laura, our parents' and now it seemed that there would be visits from other spirits to look forward to.
I remember telling William how happy and grateful I was to him and everyone.

"You have more friends than you know.
That would be a good title for a book.
You could write it".

"Yea – right" I replied dismissively.

One visitor, who periodically came, was Peter Joseph.
The first clue to his arrival, was the heat that filled the room.
In he would come, walking within his wall of heat that both John and I would feel – the nearer to me that he came, the fiercer the heat.
I soon discovered that if I mentioned the heat, or complained about the heat – the heat would become more intense.

"Positive Energy At All Times!"
was his message.

I have drawn on his message and use at as an affirmation during those times we all have, when we need the strength and will to carry out a task or work through a difficult time – and it works! Try it for yourselves.

N.B. I am writing this book in 2006 and telling you about Peter Joseph and his heat wave, I asked the question "Why did Peter Joseph choose to announce himself using heat?"

The answer came to me;
I grew up with a large framed portrait of Peter Joseph and his wife, Edith Mabel – showing them in an austere, Victorian pose - This portrait was never hung on the wall, it was always kept in our airing cupboard!!

"VERY FUNNY!"

It has only taken me 12 years to get the joke!

29th June 1994.

William; to John and myself.

"Surround yourselves in gold light.
Spirit who wish to communicate through a channel
prefer to work through gold light – for their own safety
and that of the channel.
Everyone is protected".

Qu: from John on the "opening up" procedure.

Ans:
"Kuru plays a dual role, as guide and doorkeeper.
Kuru can open your "trap door" (this is referring to the crown chakra) *to higher levels, in the same way as I can for Lynn.*
As you ask to reach a higher level – Kuru will open those levels to you.

You will find this happening more, if you firstly protect
yourself in gold light.
Do as you have been doing – asking to reach a higher
level,
Kuru will help, as she already knows, to what level you
should reach, in exactly the same way as Lynn".

Qu: "How often should I do distant healing for a
patient?"

Ans:

"You must give the healing time to work.

With the patient you have now – once a week will
suffice.
You are contact healing once a week and as you say
yourself repeatedly, it will continue to have effect..
I would suggest that three days later, after each contact
healing – if you are seeing a patient once a week".

Qu: "When healing, should I think about the patient
being well".

Ans:

"Only the inner self of the patient, knows or allows
what level of fitness they can achieve.

Their life and well-being is not in your domain.

My advice is to think of passing love and peace to your
patients – then "wander off" to a nice relaxing place,
step back and allow the patient and the healing guides
to do their work.

*In answer to your next question (*This question was pre–empted by William*) – by all means discuss the patients problems with them – give guidance and understanding to the best of your ability and that of your guide".*

John and I found these question and answer sessions invaluable and of course they were giving me more and more opportunity to practice my skills, and after each session I felt that I had learnt more.

Williams's direct communication was brilliant – straight and to the point and each time I was with him – I loved him more.

His directness – often wrapped in his sense of humour, with a hint – well, more than a hint - of sarcasm suited my own personality.

On the 5th of July 94, I asked William.

"What should I do, to prepare for work?"

Ans:

"Accept that you could receive a message at any time – be prepared to tune in at any time.
I will let Spirit through if there is a message.
A time set aside each day would be good for you – but not necessarily to receive messages.
Be prepared to receive Spirit at any time".

Qu: "Where is Armon?"

Ans:
"He's busy, but he is not far – he knows how you are".

Qu: "Is my job going to be communication?"

Ans:
"Yes, but through the communication you will also be able to work with earth energies".

Qu: "Are you enjoying working with me?"

Ans:
"I have many doors to open and you have many communications to pass on.
You will be privileged to speak to higher beings than I, and ask questions and receive answers.
You will gain valuable information to pass on to others. Your work with earth energies will play a smaller role".

I was very excited!

A couple of days later, John and I were sitting again, waiting to ask questions.
William came and then I heard the familiar:

"Hiya kid"

Armon was standing next to William; it was a while since I had seen him, so I was very pleased.

They both stood, looking at me, in silence.
My heart began to beat faster, something was wrong, maybe I had done something wrong and I was about to be told off.

Armon:

"Say goodbye to William".

I was stunned. I looked from Armon to William. The tears began to roll down my face as I repeated to John, what Armon had said.

Armon:

"Say goodbye to William".

Me: "NO"

I remember opening my eyes, folding my arms across my stomach and looking across at John, who looked as upset as myself.

I couldn't believe that this was happening, that they could do this to me – I loved them both, but now I was in such pain.

After a minute or so, I returned to William and Armon as I knew I must – but this was so hard.

Armon:
"You must say goodbye to William – he has to go".

I don't know how long I sat there, crying and sniffing. I remember looking from one of them to the other, in the hope that this was some cruel joke, but eventually I had to accept that it wasn't.

I muttered a "goodbye".
William left.
I sobbed.
And John sat in silence.

CHAPTER ELEVEN

PUT IN MY PLACE

William and I had been together for approximately 5 months, he had been my constant companion and teacher, and his leaving felt like bereavement to me.

I had no understanding of why he had left so abruptly, other than Johns' thoughts, that maybe a new guide would come and that William had other things to do.

But I didn't want a new guide – I wanted William.

I continued to listen to my music and waited – miserably – in the hope that Armon or someone, would come and help me.

It was on the 22nd July 1994, that I heard a voice say:

"Hello".

I remember sitting upright, asking for protection and raising my vibrations, in order to speak to this person – the thought running through my head, that if I wasn't quick enough, then he (I knew they were male) might get fed up and not wait for me to speak to them.
I asked him his name.

"Jose - from the Philippines".

Just as Rangu had come (described in previous chapter) – Jose told me that he had just called to say hello.

Then he left.

I was thrilled to have this short communication – it turned a miserable day, into a happy one – and I wondered if I would hear from him again.

On the 26th July, I heard: -

"No way Jose – is it God's will? – you bet it is".

I laughed at his words – what a strange character he was.
Jose then started to tell me that he was going to help me to be more sensitive to energy in general and he suggested that I begin to sit - visualise the Earth, and look for the different colours that are within it's aura.

On the 2nd August, Jose returned but there was no communication, but on the 3rd of August I had the opportunity to ask some questions, and receive some answers: -

Qu: "What is the most important thing, you have learnt in your time so far, in Spirit?"

Ans:
"Love – helping one another. Think of the earth as a whole thing, not individual countries".

Qu: "Is there a mirror of the earth, in the Universe?"

Ans: (He smiled and showed me his interlocking hands)
"There is a world that fits the same pattern as the Earth and the continents change – as do the earth's pattern. This world canbe said to be a mirror. If the two were put together, they would lock".

Qu: "What can we do to stop the Earth dying?"

Ans:
"People must learn to value one another. Only take what they need both in food and space. And give back whatever they can".

Qu: "When you say give back – in what way?"

Ans: *"By not taking – you are giving".*

Qu: "What can be done about the rainforest?"

Ans:
"It must be replaced. It is the Worlds – to be shared as a living thing – not a commodity.
All countries must now provide for the replanting.
People from different lands' cannot continue to decimate the environment of another peoples.
The peoples of the rainforests, know how to live in their environment – else they would not have been put there.
They know how to take what they need – and leave the forests to be shared by the world. They understand this.
Each peoples is put into an environment they know how to manage.
As communication has become greater, so greed has ruled. This will destroy the planet. People can move around the world and take what is not theirs. This will destroy the planet".

Qu: "What can be done to stop it?"

Ans:
"Many thousands of people must be made aware – and must be in touch with their inner selves – their spirit – which knows the truth.

That is not to say that people cannot be wealthy or powerful – but that they use their wealth and power for the greater good – mankind.
There is a place for wealth and power – indeed the world will not survive without it – and it will be given to those who will make a difference. – those bodies of people – led by their spirit and not physical drive.
These people will be the saviours of the world and its peoples.
Those who think they have the power and always will have – will have their power diminished.
The governments of the world will collapse and true leaders will take their place – and the people will follow – some from belief – others, including those deposed – from hopelessness".

Me: "William has said similar things".

Jose:
"We in spirit know this to be true and we urge you to pass the message and live your life accordingly
Your work is beginning.
I wish you well.
Our paths have crossed but once.
I shall not forget".

Me: "Neither will I".

Jose:
"We will recognise each other as we pass".

Me: "Are you leaving now?"

Jose: *"I must be prepared to go when I am bid,*
We will not say goodbye but adieu till we meet again".

During a meditation with Jose, I saw that he was building a wooden boat.

Time, I was discovering, in the spirit world, could be speeded up, slowed down or run concurrently with our own time and so it was, that in no time at all, the boat had been built and launched – in front of my eyes.

Jose invited me on board to "sail with him".

I surprised myself, when I eagerly scrambled aboard.

In my physical world – I don't like water, heights, snakes, mice … the list is endless.

Yet I was beginning to discover (with their encouragement) I was able to allow my Spirit to experience and enjoy – brilliant!

Of course, this raised the question "Where do my fears come from", because, other than sailing on a ferry around the Kyles of Bute, in Scotland, I have never been on the sea – and the only adverse event to happen on that ferry, was that someone sat on my sunglasses! (well, it annoyed me at the time!)

As for heights – well I had never fallen from one, nor had I had a bad experience on an aeroplane, in fact I had never been on one of those.

So there we were on this creaking wooden vessel (a small galleon) – sails' flapping – the sea choppy.

Suddenly, the sea calmed – it was a beautiful day, blue sky, heat from the sun – perfect.

Jose said that he had built the boat for John and I – he told me that we could get on board whenever we wanted to – he would be there to steer the boat, to take us wherever we wanted to go, adding that if the sea was too rough, we could ask for calmer water, or visa versa, depending on our mood.

Jose went on to explain, that the boat was not only a tool to be used in meditation, but it was a symbol of his wish to assist John and I on the physical path on which we were walking. In other words – he had a desire to smooth the path on which we walked - in our physical life.

I was overwhelmed by his love and generosity of Spirit, which I knew, was unconditional.
I realised that the only way I could repay this generosity, was to heed his guidance.

Regarding the boat: - Both John and I travelled on it, with him.
Successively – the same boat has been used by different guides and doorkeepers, to take me on various travels.
My last trip being – as I write now – four weeks ago – in May 2006. Twelve years after my first trip.

Jose – "Thank–you".

One person that I haven't mentioned thus far in my story, is Mr Shush.
I first met Mr Shush (he has a German name which, when he first introduced himself to me, I missed the pronunciation – so I nicknamed him Mr Shush and as he said that he didn't mind – I have continued to call him that.) in a "dream".
Mr Shush is a wise man and he still visits me now – during those times when – to put it bluntly – I need a kick up the rear end. He is a man who quickly and simply puts "everything into perspective" – he also advises me on the use of tissue salts, both for myself and for others.

On the evening of the 3rd August, Mr Shush came and
stood before me and the conversation went like this:

"Do you want to work with Spirit?"

"Yes".

"Do you know what it entails?"

"No".

"Why doesn't that bother you?"

"Because I trust".

*"You must be prepared to dedicate the rest of your life
to this work.
We don't usually ask but I will go back and report.
It makes a change for me to visit you".*

This last line was a reference to the fact that we usually
met whilst I was asleep – we had had many
conversations.

Later that night, John went to ask for distant healing for
his patients and whilst he was in meditation – he was
asked the same questions, by his guide.

Much later that night, (I was now sitting after 10
o'clock at night), Jose returned.
John had finished his meditation and we were both in
the living room.
My notebook recalls that:

I tried to project my aura – Jose tried to reflect my aura
– John tried to see it. Some success.

It was in the early evening of the next day (the 4th Aug) when I was aware of Jose's energy. I tuned in.
Jose said:
"I've got my coat on – I have been given my marching orders. It will be hours".

John and I thanked him for his communication and I also thanked him for the protection he had given me.

"All part of the service".

I asked him if there was one last thing he would like to pass on.

"Turn negatives into positives.
Have a good life".

"We cannot talk any more".

We had only known Jose a short time – yet his leaving was painful.
William, Rangu and Jose brought so much love with them – it was tangible – unconditional – never to be forgotten, and the communication that they gave us, was invaluable and also gave an interesting perspective on wider issues, notably - the future of our planet.

Feeling alone again, I filled my days with boring housework, work for our photographic business and gardening. Most of which was accompanied by music, pan – pipes being my favourite at this time.
I continued to sit to raise my vibrations, see colours and hope that someone would come to say "Hello".
I asked granddad to protect me – trusting that he would – trust was all I had, because no–one spoke to me.

These sudden periodic silences were difficult to bear, and invariably I lost my temper and patience – muttering to them sarcastically: "Well I'll just sit here shall I - is there anyone there? No – well I'll just sit here then – I'll just wait shall I?"

None of this childish ranting brought Spirit to me – but it made me feel better – albeit temporarily.

On the 12 August 1994 I noted in my book:-
Communication with my new doorkeeper.
Sioux Indian Brave called "Buffalo".

He told me to surround myself in rainbow colours and I would be under his protection.
I said it was confusing being told - gold light to rainbow light.
He said not to worry – it would get easier.
Felt floaty from the head up.
He told me to close chakras and as I did, a delivery van pulled up outside.

When I returned from receiving this communication I felt stunned and amazed, I thought – "A real Indian – a real one – as my doorkeeper!"

My mind went back in time, to two Indian dolls, one a Brave and the other a Squaw. They were on "special offer" with a certain brand of soap powder - my Mum had sent away for them.
I treasured those dolls and can still smell the leather of their clothes (yes - not plastic – real leather!)

N.B. You will all be sad to know that the dolls did not survive the ravages of time and so I no longer have them.

But – back to the Real Indian:

The next time I saw Buffalo was on the 17th of August
– my notebook reads: -
Saw Buffalos' face – long nose – square chin – feathers
dangling down the right side of head – one or two
sticking up at the back – about 40 or 50 yrs old.
Tan coloured hide trousers, and waistcoat – he is bare
chested.
He showed me a medicine man, wearing a trilby hat –
an old man – smaller than Buffalo.
I asked, "Who will be my guide? and when will we
start working?"
He said – "when the sun comes up 3 more times" he
held three fingers of his left hand up.

20/21st Aug?

I asked if there was anything I should do?
Answer: Keep talking to him and wait.

At this point – after accounting the above in my
notebook – I went back to see him.
My vibrations were nearer to his frequency and I
moved deeper into the communication – which went as
follows:

Qu: "Why is the communication distant?"

Ans
"Because we are not ready.
I speak to you because you are persistent".

Qu: "What kind of work will we be doing?"

Ans:
"Communication and earth energies".

Qu: "I am excited about this – are you?"

Ans:
"I am eager".

Qu: "Will the medicine man be helping us?"

Ans:
"He is very wise".

Qu: " Will the medicine man be my guide?"

Ans:
"He is a guide and helper".

Qu: "Yes, but will he be my guide?"

Ans:
"ENOUGH! You must wait".

Qu: "Will the communication with you be nearer when we start work?"

Ans:
"I will move closer. There is no problem. We are all just WAITING".

Qu: "Are you fed up with me asking these questions?"

Ans:
"I tire of your impatience".

Qu: "Do you understand my impatience?"

Ans

"Not really. You will be busy enough. You will not have time for these questions".

"Well I won't have a need to ask them when we are working – will I?"

Ans:

"NO. I was told of your persistence".

"I don't mean to be rude".

Ans:

"You are not rude in your manners. We will be like sparks from the same fire".

Re-reading the account of this conversation, I can't help but notice (and I'm probably not alone!) just how rude and pushy I was. What a pain in the neck!
However, it didn't deter Buffalo and I saw him the next day.

18th August 1994.

Went to see Buffalo. He was sitting, crossed legged on sandy ground. He had his back towards me.
I could see the smoke rising from a fire which was in front of him.
As I approached him from behind, he held his left hand up.
I stopped dead in my tracks, feeling as if an invisible wall had been placed in front of me.
Feeling unsure, I stood still, knowing that if I moved one step closer, I would surely bump into that wall.

Feeling like a reprimanded child – I stood and waited.
Still sitting crossed legged, and without turning to look
at me, Buffalo asked:

"What do you want?"

As he asked that question, I became aware of a bright
silvery light shining to the right, and in front of me.

Qu: "What is the name of my guide?"

The instant I had asked the question – I had the name in
my head.

"Silver Cloud" I said.
Buffalo turned, smiled and said:

"You picked that up very quickly".

My solar plexus and heart chakra were buzzing and
buzzing.

The next day (19th Aug) I felt a buzzing energy
around my head and thinking that it could be Buffalo
trying to get my attention – I tuned in.
I saw Buffalo standing with a group of other Indians –
they were talking.
I went striding over to them full of confidence.
As I approached, Buffalo suddenly turned and said (in
an irritated manner).

"What do you want?"

Feeling embarrassed, I explained that I had felt energy around my head and that I thought he might want to speak to me.

"It's not time", he snapped. *"Go back"*.

I closed down.
Surely Spirit shouldn't treat me like this? I thought.
I could almost hear the laughing of his colleagues as they turned to continue their conversation.
I was bewildered – I was also amused, knowing what a pain I could be – it served me right.
There is nothing like being put in your place, to bring you down to earth – and Buffalo did it so well, so effectively. Brilliant!

Buffalo reminded me of my English teacher, Miss Hughes and my P.E. teacher Miss Singleton – both of whom, had that ability, to silently - with just a look - make me feel as if I had, or was just about to, make a very stupid comment or action.

Buffalo and I continued to meet and by now, his energy and vibration were familiar to me, once again, I was in love with Spirit.

He always came in the same guise as described earlier, but now, as we became closer in vibration, I had touched his hand, felt the waistcoat that he wore.
I felt privileged to be with him.
His energy gave out that familiar unconditional love that comes with Spirit, and he was right when he said we would be sparks together – strangely, I enjoyed his rebukes – it made life interesting.

Suddenly, on the 26th of August 1994, I felt a familiar feeling; having my mind blanked off.

I recognised the energy – it could only be William.

He came into view.

Excitedly I listened, the tears of joy rolling down my face, as William said:

"*You must continue on your straight path*
Communication is a wonderful gift
Do what you are best at – talking".

Then I heard and saw Armon. - "*Hiya kid*".

And then they were gone.

I was overjoyed to see and hear them both.

How brilliant to see William again.

There was no other word for it, but BRILLIANT.

A lot of things were becoming brilliant in my eyes these days, including that bright light that I saw, whenever I spoke to Buffalo. It was always in the same place and getting brighter – so bright that it was now impossible to look directly at it – maybe that was Buffalos' way of forcing me to concentrate on him?

On the 4th September 1994, I was with Buffalo and felt another Spirit very close to me. Their vibrational energy was pushing me on my left side, and it kept on pushing into me, making me feel uncomfortable. I asked Buffalo, who always stood in front, and to my left – to ask the Spirit to move back. I heard him ask them, and they moved away.

Just at that moment – I saw another Indian – who I knew, was my new guide.

This was Silver Cloud

An elderly man, an Indian Chief.
Dressed in white and wearing a large, full, head-dress.
With his right arm held vertically (his left arm being held across his body) he said:

"Greetings
We will be together soon".

With that he was gone.

I was left in awe of him. His demeanour and dress, bowled me over.
Always, when in the presence of Spirit I felt privileged (even though I let my mouth "run away with me") but in the presence of Silver Cloud, not only did I feel privileged, but I recognised that his vibrations' were higher and finer than those I had been in the presence of before.

Buffalo asked me if I was *"happy now"* and for the first time – I sat down next to him.
I felt "at home" sitting on the dust, next to Buffalo and he seemed to be equally, at ease.
I turned to him and said, "You seem to be a very peaceful person". To which he replied:

"I have no need to be anything else".
 He then stood and said:
"Go back and wait".

During the next five days I continued to practice raising my vibrations and although I could occasionally feel the presence of Silver Cloud, he didn't speak directly to me until the 9th of September.

I was now feeling pressure from myself, to be disciplined in my grounding and asking for protection.
Knowing that I was impatient I was trying very hard to remember all the things that William had taught me, at the same time - listening to Buffallo – AND – trying to learn patience. Not an easy task for me!

Silver Cloud:

"We have a lot of communication to pass on
*William was bought in to open the communication channel (*me*) in such a way – so that you would enjoy it.*
Armon is pleased that you are on the right path".

In order to speak and hear Silver Cloud, I found that it took longer for me to tune in to him and I noticed that whilst we had been communicating, we seemed to be in a room – a space, that was very brightly lit.

The next day – pushing my vibrations upwards, I found myself in this same room.
Silver Cloud was standing in front of me, with Buffalo in his usual place – in front and to my left.
Silver Cloud looked towards a door, which I hadn't noticed. The door was placed in front of me and to my right, in the back wall of the room.

"Buffalo will open the door.
*They (*visiting Spirit) *will come and stand by me and speak – this is for as long as the three of us are together".*

I thought that this was brilliant – a room where we could all meet, a room where we were protected, a

room that was so bright, it made me squint, even with my eyes shut.
A place where, energetically, we would all meet.

A place towards which, I could aim my vibrations.
I knew that having merged with its vibrational energy once, my body would remember the frequency, enabling me to visit again.
I felt very fortunate, to have Buffalo and Silver Cloud as my teachers. Their attention to detail – along with clear instruction was very welcome and reassuring.
I have always responded to clear and precise language, never being one to enjoy, as others do, flowery language as found in some poetry – such words just go "over the top of my head".
I have never understood why some people use twelve words – when three would suffice!

I was feeling very happy and very excited about the future.

16th September 1994.

Morning:
Did vibrations. Felt vibrations descending – Silver Cloud.
Vibrations kept descending – I felt fatter and heavier.

Afternoon:
Did vibrations.
Went to my place.
Buffalo and Silver Cloud were there.
Felt that Armon had quietly come in – but didn't see him.
Sat crossed legged with Silver Cloud.

Silver Cloud put his hands on my feet – stayed for some time.

Stood up to leave and as I turned to say goodbye – Armon was there.

"Hiya kid – just wanted to see you all together".
I said "hello" and "thankyou".
He left – I left.

It was a lovely experience to sit with Silver Cloud and I felt that he had been grounding me – just as William had done, and I knew that this grounding would strengthen our partnership – in fact I could feel the link between us growing stronger as we had sat.

I felt that I had known Silver Cloud for a long time, that our energies were in harmony; the very same feelings that I experienced when I was in the company of Armon and the rest of my family, William, Rangu and Jose.

The unconditional love that they permeate and also – because we meet on a truly vibrational level – our heightened senses, when combined, means that nothing - in my experience - whilst we are in the physical form, can totally replicate that feeling of "oneness".

CHAPTER TWELVE

SAY IT .... AS IS

At the same time as all these wonderful things were happening, John and I were continuing to be frustrated by the financial aspect of our business. As with many small businesses, we had no difficulty in finding the work, it was chasing the monies owed that was becoming a constant concern. However, Silver Cloud advised me that:

"Physical matters should be put aside".

and:

"The physical path should not be allowed to interfere with the Spiritual path".

In the same communication and referring to any message I would receive for someone, he also warned:

"If you do not pass on ALL the message – I will not speak".

I had already been tested on my ability to trust my communication and to pass on a message as given, one evening at Tracy and Jon's months ago: - It was there that I received a communication from the Grandmother of one of the people also present. The grandmother's communication was;

"Tell her that the pills won't work – she mustn't do it".

This message was the first message that I had been asked to pass in my work for spirit and I remember how uncomfortable I felt being asked to pass it on. I felt like an intruder into her private life, I knew the message was correct and yet I felt very uncomfortable in this situation. I had only exchanged a few words with her – up until now.

I know I began to fidget in my chair, I remember asking for some other "nice" message to be passed instead – I was resisting passing on what the grandmother had said and at the same time I knew that I must.

I relayed the message to her.

She instantly, completely dismissed the message, saying that it made no sense to her at all, adding that she was upset with me for passing such a message on to her, and then she walked away.

I was upset myself - but I also knew that the message was correct.

It would be about a month later, when Jon gave me a message from her which was that; she was sorry for reacting angrily, the message had come as a shock to her and she had indeed contemplated taking pills, she added that the message had helped convince her not to.

I was relieved – for both of us!

Writing down all the communication was, by now, becoming quite difficult.

Silver Cloud spoke at a normal speed – I either repeated it – or delivered the communication directly to John – who in turn hastily wrote in the notebook.

Alternatively, if I was on my own with Silver Cloud, Buffalo or someone else, I would write the notebook up after the communication had finished.
So John and I decided to ask Silver Cloud if we could use a tape recorder.
He replied:

"Yes – nothing can be distorted.
 You may hear my voice on a tape one day".

So it was, that from now on, all the communication was taped. And I would spend as long as it took, the next day, transcribing the tape.

On the 18th September 1994, which happens to be my Dads' birthday, Silver Cloud surprised me by repeating the title for a book that William had given me – "More Friends than you know".

"That is a good title for your book" he said.

I wondered why they kept going on about me writing a book, at the same time I recalled how, during a reading with Tracy, she said to me that my Dad told her that I would write a book.

From my experience of Spirit I had come into contact with, thus far, I knew that many of them had a sense of humour... this book talk, was their way of having some fun at my expense – "very funny!"

One question that kept popping into my mind, was the question of the approximate age Spirit seemed to be when I saw them? Why, when I saw Jose, did he appear to me as a young man (20s) – when, during one conversation we had had, he told me that he was 46yrs old when he died?

Why, during a conversation with my mother, did she change her appearance – right before my eyes: One second she looked like my Mum (approximately the same age as when she died – only looking happy and healthy) and then I watched in amazement as she metamorphosised into her early twenties. And then disappear.

Whilst tuning in to Silver Cloud, I had occasionally glimpsed the face of a younger man and so one day I asked him if Spirit did indeed choose to appear at a certain age – and if so – why did he (Silver Cloud) appear now as an older man.

He answered, saying – Yes, the younger face I had seen was indeed him at a younger age – and he went on to say that he chose to appear as an older man because it was later on in his life time, that he received most respect.

My conclusion being that spirit could choose an age in their life when they were most happy – but having said that, I also understood that to them – the physical form was no longer relevant - which raised another question; "Was their projection of their physical form mainly for my benefit?"

This question went unasked – I realised that to allow myself to become bogged down in asking endless questions, I ran the risk of going round in circles. The endless questions would side track me from receiving the communication that they chose to pass – anyway, I reasoned, there was the strong possibility that when

I passed over into the Spirit world – I would "remember" the answers myself.

I was loving meeting with Silver Cloud and Buffalo in my place and the more frequently that I went, the easier it was to arrive there.

Silver Cloud suggested that I use music when raising my vibrations and opening up to Spirit. I had avoided using music during times of communication as my tendency to "sing along" interfered with the serious business of receiving communication. Thus began the challenge of hearing and using the music through my body – whilst - listening and communicating with spirit. Knowing, that if I allowed my concentration to drift – a swift rebuke would surely follow.

It was as I arrived at my place one day, that I saw Peter Joseph standing there with Trampas at his feet.

I was thrilled to bits to see them.

"Look at me!" commanded Silver Cloud.

Everytime I glanced over to Peter Joseph and my beloved Old English Sheepdog – I heard the same command.

"Look at me".

I was jolted into remembering the procedure that Silver Cloud had explained to me – how Buffalo would let someone come in, how they would stand by Silver Cloud and then they would pass their communication. In other words – Discipline.

I stood in front of Silver Cloud and said hello – he acknowledged me with a slight nod of his head and extended his right arm towards Peter Joseph – inviting him to come and stand in front of me - which he did – with Trampas obediently walking alongside. I recall thinking that both Trampas and myself were attending the same obedience class – he had never walked to heel for me and I had never stood quietly for him.

Peter Joseph, austere as always, began by saying that Trampas was still herding chickens. (I will tell that story further on down the chapter). He then announced that he was moving on.

He said that he was going to teach the children in a school and that he would be taking Trampas with him, adding, with a wry smile, that Trampas was very disobedient but nonetheless, he was going to be a "pat dog".

I had been shown – during one of my nightly excursions – a nursery containing cots, in which were many infants. Not all of them were happily gurgling away to themselves, but some crying for attention. That attention was given by ladies, dressed in the traditional garb of nurses, who quietly and calmly went about their duties – seeming oblivious to the din. The nursery is a happy place – a serenity hanging in the air, amidst the noise and activity – a place of developing Spirit.

I had also met a small group of children, when they visited John and myself as we sat in our living room. These children were children of the Jewish Holocaust. Tears streamed down my face as, standing before me, one of them delivered their joint message;

"Never forget the children".

Peter then announced his departure and as he walked away, Trampas bounded along in front of him.

This was the Trampas I knew, eager for the next game – whatever that would be - excited and anticipating the attention that was about to be bestowed on him, and that, he would bestow on others.

I remember cringing as I silently called to Trampas's rear end – "Be careful Trampas – don't knock them over!"

Silver Cloud said;
"That was a surprise for you
That dog would not make a hunter, if he found a
rabbit, he would play with it
I am not used to pets but I can see the advantage of
having a friend – but such a hairy one?
Buffalo is covered in dog hair!

Peter Joseph speaks plainly – the children will
understand and grow to love him, they can use the dog
as a cushion".

He continued with;

"You are a totem pole – you are our front
You must relay the messages in a true form
You must show no harm to anyone
These are the rules.
If you follow the rules, many evolved spirits will use
you as a channel – that is why you have been asked to
dedicate the rest of your time to be used as a channel.
This explanation is the basis on which you will conduct
the rest of your life".

"I thank you ".

During the same communication, Silver Cloud
continued: -

*"Healers are conductors – they conduct the healing
energy from their guides and helpers around them
A conductor must keep in time with the orchestra.
Clever use of English!
A healer is a brilliant channel in the sense that he lights
up – to conduct
There is an element of wit, is there not?"*

*"So much good work can be done through healing, as
you know – not just physically.
Healing a body – that is merely a scratch on the
surface – the symptom is in the mind – the healing
opens the mind, if done correctly, with guidance and
responsibility".*

*"Healing guides have spent a life time as physicians,
surgeons and counsellors – and, such is their
dedication, that when their life on earth is past, they
continue to work in Spirit, through the healing
conductor".*

*"The dedication of these people is tremendous, as they
have to study continuously, so that they are aware of
changing medical factors".*

"It is an eternity of dedication".

*"There will be more on these subjects but you both now
are aware of the task in front of you.
A task you take on with a light heart
As you embark further down your spiritual path – your
physical load will become lighter".*

"That is a reality."

"Have faith – enjoy every small delight and the burden will lift.
I know this to be true – Believe".

To me:
"You may go".

John and I:
"Thankyou".

"Tomorrow is another day".

Before I move on to the next day's communication, I will now tell the chicken herding story.

During my early twenties I spent a couple of years working with horses and with my bosses' permission, I used to take Trampas to work with me.
The smallholding where I worked was owned by the Grandfather of my boss, and Trampas loved "going to work".
It provided a constant source of entertainment.
The manure heap was a favourite, supplying not only heat in winter, but an opportunity for a snack or two – that of course, was only after the supply of sponges had temporarily run out – for some reason, Trampas thought that the sponges we used would be of more use to us, in bite size pieces, he particularly loved the ones that were used to clean the tack and were covered in oil or saddle soap.
I lost count of the number of sponges I replaced.

When playing with humans, Trampas would play rough, he had an uncanny knack of jumping up at men and flicking his foot upwards, catching any unsuspecting male, where it hurts most. If for any reason we sat on the floor, he would pounce – delivering a right hook across your face as he bounded in, which had the effect of knocking you backwards and then as you lay in the prone position, he would sit on you - staring deeply into your eyes as if to say "got ya".

.

But on the smallholding, it was his fellow animals that delighted him most.

He would go to join the horses that were kept in the field and graze along side them, and when the cat had a litter of kittens, his maternal, feminine side, emerged.

As the kittens began to explore their surroundings, Trampas took on the job of nanny – gently picking a kitten up, walking across the yard, and depositing the said kitten in what he must have deemed to be a safer place. Of course as any mother cat would tell you, keeping inquisitive kittens in one safe place, and all together, is a thankless task. But it didn't stop Trampas trying and I think the mother cat was glad to have a "baby sitter" because she never objected. Which is more than can be said of "Granddad": -

"Tell that dog to leave those b------y kittens alone" he would shout.

And this leads me to the chickens.

"Granddad" had a small flock of laying chickens, which, in the daytime, were free range.

Round the yard they went, scratching away, minding their own business. However, Trampas had other ideas. For some reason he thought that they would be safer in a group (just like the kittens) and so he would round them up, but being really security conscious his aim was to put them back in their shed.

This action of course, upset the chickens – not to mention the cockerel, and they would begin to squawk. This squawking alerted not only myself, but Granddad and before I had time to grab the dog, I would hear "Tell that dog to leave those B-----dy chickens alone!"

You would expect to hear - after reading about the antics of Trampas - that he would have been banned from the yard, but that was not the case because you see, Trampas knew just how far he could push a human being.

He often plodded round after Granddad, gently nuzzling his drooped hand in companionship – peering up at him, with those appealing blue eyes - and - he never did anything to upset Grandmother. Clever eh!

I continued to take Trampas to work with me, that is, until the day when:

My boss, her husband, myself, along with Trampas and a Jack Russel, (which belonged to her Granddad), were walking down the lane one afternoon. We were going to the field, to fetch two of the horses in for the night.

We saw car came towards us and we all moved onto the grass verge, taking the dogs with us. The car driver deliberately swerved towards Trampas and caught him on his hip with the bumper of the car.

The driver sped off.

Trampas turned and ran back to the yard, where he hid in an open stable.

Fortunately, he was not badly hurt, but for the first, and only time – I saw fear in his eyes.

My memory took me back to the day Moss had been killed, and I was filled with the horror of what could have been the outcome that day.

We had all had a scare as a result of this incident, and so John and I decided that Trampas would now have to stay at home. As he was only 18months old, we also decided to get him a friend – which is when we got Muppet. Muppet was a present from John's mum, Elsie, and when she came to see just what she had bought for us – the three month old Muppet - with his hairy snout, that resembled a bottle cleaner – refused to come out from under the settee.

Sadly – the Jack Russell was run over on the same road, later that year.
The driver did not stop.

!9th **September 1994.** Afternoon. Saw Buffalo.

Qu: "Buffalo, what do you do when you are not working with me?"

Ans:
"Read. Books appear in my mind and I also see historical events".

Me: "I wish I could have studied for my exams like that – I would have passed more".

Ans:
"You people judge one another by pieces of paper, not what is inside".

Me: "I do that – judge?"

Ans
"You will learn gentler ways".

Qu: "Do you enjoy working with Silver Cloud?"

Ans:
"It is an honour".

Expecting to see and hear from Silver Cloud that same evening, I was surprised when, upon arrival in my place, I saw a gentleman dressed in a dark suit (circa English – late 1800s – early 1900) standing in front of me.

I barely had a second to glance at Buffalo in an effort to check with him that it was right for me to tune into this person, when…

"Good Evening" he boomed.
"I am Harold Bennet, Eminent physician".

The strength of this gentleman's character swept towards me – the type of person who commanded attention and I felt rather awe struck in his presence.

Addressing himself to John he continued:

"I worked in the slum areas of London, where there was much sickness and disease – brought about by poor conditions and malnutrition and a degeneration of society".

"I am working with you because you are in contact with lower classes – not fashionable terminology – but used now …… lower classes in the respect……. dealing with people who's illnesses'…. are brought about by degeneration of circumstance. I continue my work in Spirit".

"I am sorry – I am confusing myself – I am not used to communicating."

"As I worked in the physical world with the same type of person. There are now many more poor people than ever before, so there is plenty of work to be done".

"I worked hard in my physical life to my own detriment and now I find to my great joy, I can work hard consistently. And I will work you hard".

"I have enjoyed communicating. You know that I am here".

"I will take my leave".

"Good Evening".

Buffalo:
"He is a very clever man, unfortunately his dedication and hard work means he lacks social skills.
Silver Cloud is not here but Harold Bennet was on the list – you certainly know he has called".

It was amazing for me to feel the energy of Harold Bennet, as I was delivering his communication, I was bristling – feeling his sense of urgency and self importance and his message was delivered in the same tone – leaving John and I grateful for his communication – but speechless.

Mr Bennet still occasionally works with John, some twelve years later – he is still brusque at times, he has a sense of humour, speaks plainly and is one, I personally ask for, when I feel confused. Mr Bennet makes things simple – Oh – he also likes Jazz music – UGH!

The next day, on arriving at my place, Silver Cloud invited myself and Buffalo to sit on the floor with him. I was told to raise my vibrations again and as I did so I could feel myself becoming lighter and lighter, it felt as though the organs inside my body were shaking and my head was elongating and reaching ever upwards.
Silver Cloud then told me ask *"that my energy be joined with theirs"*.
As I asked for this I had a sense of "oneness" with them. Silver Cloud then told me to ask Buffalo to step away, which I did, and as Buffalo stood and began to withdraw from the circle I felt his energy disentangle and draw away,
Silver Cloud then told me to lower my vibrations and go back.

I was still buzzing as I "came back" into our living room – still buzzing and trying to lower my vibrations.
When John arrived home later that day, I told him what had happened. "It must have blown your socks off," he said, by way of instant reply, I heard Buffalo say, *"Blow our feathers off"*.

That evening, on arriving at my "place", I saw that Silver Cloud was sitting and meditating – I withdrew.
Later, Silver Cloud explained that he was meditating and communicating with HIS guide – White Cloud - as he had done when he lived in the physical world.
He went on to explain that through his meditations, he foresaw the death of his own peoples, a burden which *"Hung heavy in my heart"*. He added that his Spirit guides had told him that the events which would lead to their deaths would have to take place, and further more, that he must lead them to their deaths.

As Silver Cloud spoke, I could feel a little of his pain
and sadness - it was still tangible - making me feel
very humble.
I realised, in that instant, that I had been so wrapped up
in my development and what "they" were going to give
and teach me, so caught up in the me, me, me syndrome
and the "what next?", so excited – that I had not given
much thought to the events and experiences that "they"
had, had – experiences - which had driven these spirits,
to choose to return to the earth plane as guides,
doorkeepers, friends and acquaintances, to assist myself
and many, many other people – unconditionally.

As I stood and absorbed these revelations, I felt my
vibrations lifting higher. I heard the words:

*"Silver Cloud is a VERY spiritual man, deserving of
GREAT RESPECT".*

I knew that these words had come from White Cloud,
and I replied silently and with sincerity.

"It is a privilege to speak with you – Thank you".

In some odd way, I felt as though I had grown up.

I knew that this session wasn't over and on my return to
my place I was met by a man who said his name was
Tahula. Buffalo said that he didn't think Tahula would
speak, as he wasn't sure of the channel (me). Buffalo
then went on to explain that Tahula was looking for a
channel to communicate through.
I recall how Tahula stood looking at me in silence and I
stood (although I was actually sitting in my favourite
armchair) shuffling my feet, not knowing what to do.
To break the silence, Buffalo said;

"*Did you know that chestnuts are poisonous when small? Like Bach flowers – they have got to be given in the right proportions.*
That's why squirrels don't eat them – they must wait".

"*I will take my leave now.*
*He (*Tahula) *will speak to Silver Cloud".*

"*Wait".*

Once again I returned to the living room and waited.

After a few minutes I felt that it was time for me to return – Silver Cloud was waiting:

"*As you can see, he (*Tahula) *has gone – Tahula, yes you have got the name correctly.*

He is looking for a channel but will not used an un-proved one, which I feel, at this moment in time is his loss.
He has not yet found a channel to transmit his words truly..
He is a healing guide and a little suspicious of the medium.
He will need proof of your mediumship but assures me that he will watch our progress.
He also knows that many questions will arise from his transmissions and would prefer his transmission was at a time when the healer is present to ask his own questions.
This will be good experience for you and will test your ability".

"*I hear Buffalo has been visiting – imparting his wisdom – he has aspirations I think, to be a guide*

195

*himself one day – but he has much work to do and will
not be released.
We will keep him busy".*

*"I have waited years to have my own channel – it is
carefully planned.
You have much work to do – you must keep practising
the vibrations, as they are the key.
I have work to do in this matter and when our
vibrations finally and totally meet – I will speak".*

*"I tire, as you tire
Our communication is over for the day.
Goodnight".*

I had heard the name Tahula before – a healer friend of
ours had said that a medium had given this name, as the
name of his guide.

Around this time, Hems, a good friend of ours, offered
John healing for his neck problems – which he'd had
for years.

John had, for several years, ridden a succession of
different motor bikes. During that time, he'd had minor
mishaps, but nothing serious. However, on day, he was
involved in a major incident - during which, he was
knocked off his bike and dragged along the road.

John received trauma to his neck and throat (his head
was snatched backwards – and his helmet split into two
pieces) and also trauma to his back, chest (his sternum
was broken), ribs, shoulders, arms and legs.
Although John had made a good recovery initially – his
back and neck – the vertebrae having collapsed –
continually caused pain. So much pain - that one day

during the late 80s – he collapsed. John was off work for 3 months, receiving physiotherapy. The medical diagnosis was that John would eventually become "wheelchair bound". This very bleak prognosis hung over us like a dark cloud.

The offer of healing from our friend, at a time when John was once more, in a lot of pain – was very welcome.

After the first healing session, John's pain increased, he was in agony. I was scared – wondering if he would collapse again.

However, John was absolutely convinced that the healing was helping, he was convinced that the added pain was a good sign, he knew that he was being healed, and he had no hesitation in carrying on with the sessions.

The change in John's degree of fitness soon became apparent. His back became straighter, he could hold his head up straight, and the movement returned in both his neck and back - as the vertebrae were released and realigned. The pain went away.

John has remained well as the years have gone on. That bleak diagnosis left behind.

We will always be grateful to Hems and his guides – grateful to Spirit for the healing energy – grateful for the freedom that energy has allowed.

I return now, to the communication:

As soon as Tahula announced his name, I was given the "link" in my head which led directly to his channel.

I was beginning to understand further, the never ending links between our Spirit and our physical beings friends.

As Silver Cloud would say;

"If I don't know – I know a man who does – I will see if I can find him".

I also understand that there are varied reasons as to why, sometimes, communication for someone cannot be passed through me – which is why I have no hesitation in saying to someone; "I'm sorry, I am not the one to help you".
I am pleased to say that Tahula did use me as a communication channel and his communication began the "question and answer" system way of working, that works so well.

On the 22nd September 1994, Angela came into our lives.

I had felt an energy come and stand before me and when I tuned in to the vibration, I saw this little girl.
She seemed to be a shy girl – looking down at her feet in a shy, coy manner, she was holding a doll which wore a pointed hat. She was a pretty blonde haired child and when I asked her name, she replied boldly:

"Angela – I want to tell mummy that I am here – that I am alright".

Again, I felt the links – the links told me the first name of her mother, the reason why Angela was in the Spirit world and also the name of the person to whom I would have to pass this message on to, I did not know the mother personally.

As I received these links, I was aware that Angela knew that I had received them – she relaxed with a sigh, and left.

I immediately went to my place to see Silver Cloud and found him standing holding Angela's doll.
Handing the doll over to me, he said,

"The doll is a symbol of the children you will help".
.

I told him that I felt the burden of passing this message on, and felt that I, and the other messenger, would be intruding into someone's private life - maybe they didn't want to know about Angela?
I had not yet grasped the concept that these personal messages were timely - I had to trust that whenever Spirit passed a message on to me, and whatever or however obscure that message might seem to be to me – I had a duty to pass it on.

As Silver Cloud would say:

"Just say it – As Is"

CHAPTER THIRTEEN

ONWARDS AND UPWARDS.

A s I begin this chapter, I need to explain to you, the meanings of two phrases, which you will be reading.

Raised vibrations;
> The act of raising vibrations is a disciplined task which entails;
> Sitting and calming myself – clearing or ignoring those everyday – often mundane - thoughts that run through my mind.
> Grounding – feeling my connection with the earth energies. (I was still using the root visualisation).
> Asking for protection from my doorkeeper – and NOT proceeding until I see, feel, or sense my doorkeepers' presence, agreement and readiness.

Returned to my chair:
> Thanking Spirit for their protection, guidance and communication.
> Lowering my vibrations by closing down my chakras and grounding the energy.
> Grounding until I know that I am re-connected to the earth – this can take more than one attempt.

During the narrative, I will use these phrases, almost like a "post script", as if they are unimportant – that could not be further from the truth.

Raised vibrations and returned to my chair are the procedures - simply and patiently taught to me by my Spirit guides - that are paramount to my work.

23rd September 1994.

Went to my "place" and saw it was a green field, surrounded by hedges. (Just like the one I had played in as a child – the field that William had sent me back to). As there was no one there I left and returned one and a half hours later.

This time I saw Buffalo, the field had gone and in its' place was my usual, brighter than bright place.
I explained to Buffalo (as if he didn't know) that I had been earlier, and that I had found myself in a field, but as there hadn't been anyone else there, I had left.

"We were closed for lunch" he replied.

I don't know if you, the reader, can imagine yourselves, standing in front of an American Indian, complete with sticky out feathers, telling you that he had gone out to lunch.
I don't know what you would have said – but I said – "Oh" - and swiftly moved on.

"What have you been doing?" I asked.

Buffalo leaned towards me, smiling. He reached out and gently touched my face as I smiled back at him.

"That's none of your business" he replied.

There had never been many times in my life so far, when I had been stuck for words – unable to give some retort – unable to think of another question to ask – and being British, resorting to comments on the weather – but Buffalo could "stop me dead in my tracks" with his replies.

It was with much relief, that I suddenly noticed Mr Shush – he was sitting behind a desk, turning the pages of a large, leather bound book.

I began to walk towards him and as I did so, he closed the book that was now in his hands.

When I reached the desk, I saw that the book had disappeared and in its' place, he was holding a large diamond shaped crystal.

Mr Shush held the crystal out towards me and asked me to look into it.

As I peered at the crystal, I saw many faces, appearing and disappearing and as I continued to look, the crystal turned into a white silk square, which immediately turned into a white dove, which instantly flew out of his hands, and also disappeared.

It was a moment of magic, a moment in which I quietly, asked Mr Shush where I knew him from, his reply was - we had known one another in a previous life and now;

"*We meet again*".

I also asked if he had any advice for me.

"*Be true*".

And with that, he too disappeared.

In a state of complete calm and happiness, I walked over to Buffalo, who had been observing the magic moment.

I said that I could feel Silver Cloud around but I couldn't see him.

"Silver Cloud is watching – even if you can't see him", he explained.

With that, Buffalo disappeared for the briefest of moments and re-appeared – flying round the room – like a kite that had been released from its' string – on a very windy day.

Not daring to move, I stood and watched, and felt the air move around me as Buffalo swept by.
He landed softly at my feet, with not a feather out of place.

Not knowing what to say, I moved swiftly on with a question on John's behalf. John wanted an explanation to an event that had happened during the previous night, whilst he had been asleep.

Briefly, John had been aware of a death caused by, what he suspected, was an accident, and although John knew it was not himself who was dying, he had been aware of the pain and emotions of that death.
On waking, John obviously needed some understanding of what had happened.
I could only confirm that John had been making whimpering and moaning noises during his sleep and had been very restless.

Buffalo replied;

"Your request has been noted".

That was the end of this session.

By now, the daily evening sessions began at 11pm; this allotted time allowed for distant healing to be done at 10pm, plus the all-important cup of tea afterwards.
These sessions, depending on my ability and the number of "visitors" combined with the length of the communication – could last for up to 4hrs. To this day, my preference is to work in the early hours of the morning.

The evening of the same day, I once again raised my vibrations, this time with John in attendance.

Silver Cloud introduced me to a gentleman who was standing with him;

"This is Mr White" He explained.

There was no more communication and I lowered my vibrations and returned into myself, knowing that I must raise my vibrations again in order to "tune into" the vibrations of Mr White.

On returning to my "place", Mr White introduced himself by name – Albert White, and said that he had a message for John.
I must point out here that in order to receive his communication, it took me a few minutes to align myself with his vibrations. Each individual Spirit energy vibrated slightly differently than another; feeling to me, as though they were either very close, or further away from me. Also; the personality of each individual shone through their vibrations. The length of

time it took me to communicate with them, depended on my physical reaction to that personality; just as in the physical world, there are some people I judge it, to be easy in their company, and some, I do not.

The first part of the following communication shows how I related the communication to John – then you will see that, as I became more attuned to Mr White – the communication develops into direct communication between Mr White and John.

Albert White began his communication by explaining that he was a receiver of those passing over into the Spirit world, and that on the previous night, a man had died as a result of an accident, and this had been the death that John was aware of.

He then went on to say that Laura (see chapter 9) was, as he described her, a scout. Further explaining that Laura assisted people, particularly those who were passing over suddenly, as the result of an accident.

He said that he, Mr White, had a department within the Spirit world especially for those people, and further – how they arrived in deep shock, and needed special care.
He went on to say that what had happened to John, the previous night would not be a regular occurrence, but was a further example of healing work, adding, that it had been an actual person that had passed over last night - it was not play acting.

John;
Qu: "What was my role, did I just witness it?"

Ans:
"You took part in it – the guiding of the Spirit".

John: "From my point of view, I felt as if I was that person".

Ans:
"But you weren't hurt were you?"

Qu: "Will Laura still be with me? Will we be doing similar work?"

Ans:
"Laura has been around you for a long while".

John: "I owe her my apologies for not recognising her".

Ans:
"Laura has changed – we do not expect you to instantly recognise us. Of course Laura will be with you".

The reference here to Laura changing, is a reference to the fact that Laura, was a young woman, no longer the child.

Qu: "Is there another role that Laura will be playing in any healing – anything specifically?"

Ans:
"She will be there with the healing with children".

John: "She mentioned that last time we spoke"

Mr White:
"Last nights occurrence is something that won't happen very often. Has it happened before?"

John: "Yes – I do appreciate being made aware of it last night".

Mr White:
"It is a very important job. It is something you will learn more of, during astral travelling".

John: "Is there any way I can improve that side of what I'm doing?"

Ans:
"You will be guided. It is not something that can be taught - certainly not during waking hours. This is an occurrence that takes place during sleeping hours".

"I will speak again and I hope the channel is more organised next time".

"Goodnight".

Just when I thought that I might, just might, have done a good job of work – I was brought down to earth with Mr Whites' next to last sentence.
The reference to my lack of organisation referred to the fact that – just as Mr White began to speak, the tape on my machine ran out - if you remember I had been permission to tape these messages.
I had hastily inserted a new tape as quickly as I could, but obviously not quick enough.

The communication continued, this time from Silver Cloud:

"You delivered the communication – BUT – people do not expect to wait and repeat themselves, whilst you organise yourself".

"The context of the message was correct

You do realise that you are now working? You must tape all messages and be professional".

Feeling suitably admonished and in an attempt to redeem myself, with the added bonus (hopefully) of diverting Silver Clouds' attention away from tutting and shaking his head at me, I swiftly moved on.
I asked Silver Cloud for his explanation of why and how the event of this accident and subsequent death, combined with Johns' part in it – took place.

Silver Cloud:
"You have heard the phrase, keeping body and soul together? – this is ensuring that the soul and spirit arrive at the same time – important on the occasion of a sudden passing.
It is easier for the deceased, if the soul and the spirit arrive at the same time – so that when they awake, they think they are physical. Less traumatising".

John: "How did my being there help that?"

Ans:
"You kept the two together – protected it".

Qu; "Who is Mr White?"

Ans:
"A G.P. who had worked in hospitals in an earlier career. He has chosen to work with trauma cases. This work is of great value and has very quick results of recovery. He is somewhat of an expert in this field and his experience as a G.P. has given him what you would call, the bedside manner".

"Laura is a wonderful lady – you knew her as a child and now you will know her as she is – she has retained her sense of fun.
She still appears to you as the "cold on the legs" and will work with you during sleeping hours – but – also, as you will understand – has a great love of children and therefore will work as a healing guide when you are working with children".

"Do not forget that healing is not just opening as the healing channel, but healing is talking and reaching out. You could do a lot of good work with autistic children".

"Be open to all subtle changes".

"End of transmission".

Silver Cloud now turned his attention back to myself:

"Now you".

"What was so difficult about that?"

"Did it not flow better?" (The new tape was working without a hitch).

"I hope you have learnt a valuable lesson".

"Now go my child".

As I lowered my vibrations, I could see Buffalo standing and wagging his finger at me, in a side to side motion, just as a parent does to its' defiant toddler who has already been told "NO", the only difference being that Buffalo was smirking and smiling as he did it!

The next morning I raised my vibrations and went to my "place" only to find that there was a pair of curtains drawn across the entrance.

Buffalos' head appeared from behind the curtains and he said:

"You can't come in".

Then he disappeared behind the curtains, leaving me with no option than to leave.

Does it sound crazy to you, when I say that I was really enjoying (on the whole) being treated this way. Yes! It could be irritating and confusing at times but mostly – it just made me laugh.

That evening (24thSeptember 1994), John and I sat in our living room - and I returned to my "place". On my arrival I saw – Kuru and a Japanese Samurai Warrior, who introduced himself as Katamoro.
The warrior began to speak and pass his message, but I was struggling to concentrate. His startling appearance had shocked me, his energy and persona was overwhelming me.
I blocked the message and returned to the haven of my chair.

The sight of this warrior had sent my vibrations tumbling (or rather; I had allowed that to happen) and my temperature soaring.
Back in my chair and flapping my right hand quickly in front of my face in a desperate bid to cool and calm myself down - I turned to John and said;

"There's this Samurai Warrior – dressed in all that black gear! He looks scary! - Oooh! - I'll have to calm down".

"I'll have to go back!"

I must note here, that, apart from the garb of a Samurai, that I recognised from pictures in books – I instantaneously KNEW, that a Samurai Warrior was standing in front of me:

Our Spirit, when freed from of our mind – recognises another Spirit instantly.
Our Spirit, when freed from our mind – receives information – instantaneously.

However – I was just beginning – and a Samurai Warrior, in full "dress", complete with VERY BIG SWORD! – was un-nerving.

Having got over the initial shock, and feeling calmer, I returned to my "place".
The warrior was still there but as I looked at him, his clothing changed into a white Judo suit, and around his waist, the warrior was wearing a long sash, which had Japanese writing on it.
The change of clothes immediately made me feel more at ease.
I concentrated on raising my vibrations, to attune with his.

"*I will appear in the white suit*" he stated, in a kindly, gentle way.

A combination of, my feelings of awe at being in his presence, and his fine, and high vibrations – resulted in me reverting to – hearing his communication – then passing the communication on to John.

The warrior introduced himself once more, as Katamoro.
He went on to say that he would rather have been a healer, than a warrior.
He described himself as a magician.
Adding that he was now – John's healing guide.

At this moment, Kuru stepped forward and explained that John would feel Katamoro, touch his neck, in the same place as she did, adding, jokingly, that she and Katamoro were the same height.
John confirmed that Kuru did announce her presence by touching his neck – always in the same place.

Kuru then said that

"The healing would reach new dimensions".

With that – Kuru stepped back – saying to John;

"We will meet again".

Kuru left.

Katamoro continued, by telling how he had been watching John and that he was pleased to note his dedication, adding that he (Katamoro) would now be called – Kato.

Along with the excitement of meeting Kato, the feeling of loss - as Kuru left – was tangible.

Silver Cloud moved forward into my vision. He spoke quietly – seeming to reflect our mood of change and loss:

Kato, he said, was a very spiritual being – a magician.

With those words - the head of a yellow chrysanthemum appeared, floating in the air – it turned into a butterfly – and the butterfly flew away.

Once again, I returned to my chair. I needed a break; I needed to ground the energy that was around me.
Kuru had gone – and I needed a few minutes to digest that news, I needed to talk through the communication with John – they were his guides, I wanted to know how he felt about this sudden change.

After several minutes discussion and mindful that I had left my "place" abruptly, I raised my vibrations again and returned to my "place" – to be met by an incandescent Silver Cloud.

"WHY DID YOU NOT PASS THE MESSAGE THE FIRST TIME!"

"DID YOU NOT UNDERSTAND THE HIGH LEVEL OF VIBRATION TO WHICH YOU WERE TUNED IN TO!"

He was VERY cross; he stamped one foot hard on the ground and clapped his hands in rhythm with his words.

My mind flipped back to the time when I was about 7 or 8yrs old – when a teacher had physically taken hold of my arms and shaken me until my teeth rattled - the reason for her anger being that I had failed to spell a word correctly during an oral spelling test.

I realised that I had kept Kato waiting, I realised that I had let my fears and subsequent actions interrupt the proceedings and I was VERY sorry.
I told Silver Cloud so.

I judged that Silver Clouds' lengthy silence after my apology meant that he had nothing more to add, and so I began to lower my vibrations and close my chakras.

"Can you still hear me?" he asked as I descended.

"Yes" I replied.

I returned to my chair and told John what had happened. (John spent hours sitting in his chair – waiting!)

Feeling the familiar energy of Silver Cloud descending on me, I closed my eyes and waited:

"White Cloud has reminded me that I did not lead my people by shouting – but by quiet guidance and knowledge".

"I am sorry – I was excited for you – for you to meet Katamoro".

"I was, carried away".

"No messages were lost – it was just sloppy!"

At this point, the audiotape that John had quickly turned back on again – ran out.

I have no entry in my notebook for the next day (25th), I must have decided to have a day off – it is not beyond the realms of possibility that I was sulking – however on the morning of 26th September, I noted:

Did vibrations – felt pain in my ear, and on the right side of my face.
Came back to my chair.

Later.

Did vibrations. Silver Cloud friendly.

Evening.

Silver Cloud is standing, holding a long pole which has feathers attached to it.

He motions – to tell me to wait – then he waves to me.

I walk towards him.

I ask:

"Are we going to work tonight?"

"There is a whole universe our there – behind my door. We have plenty of time".

"I will send Buffalo for you".

At this point, I felt a lot more energy around me – I felt my inner vibrations lifting.

N.B. Each time that I experienced my vibrations lifting and quickening, it resulted in my feeling sick and/or dizzy. I would ask for protection and "grounding" - grounding myself, but needing their help. I knew that grounding was the key, to enable my vibrations to lift. I was learning to put these physical symptoms aside – I knew that I had to work through them – and not give up. These exercises took time, anything from, half an hour - to repeatedly trying, on and off, for a whole day, and on some occasions, into the next day.

"You must lift your vibrations, to the highest order – till you are one of us".

"You have a long way to go".

I followed Silver Clouds' instructions and as my vibrations lifted, I clearly saw Silver Clouds' face.
He removed a feather from his headdress and silently, offering it to me as a gift - he laid it on the floor of my "place".

The face that I was looking at, was the face of a younger Silver Cloud.
His vibration remained the same – that familiar one.

I asked – "Why am I seeing the younger Silver Cloud".

He replied:

"The older Silver Cloud – who was waving to you – was waving "Goodbye".

Shortly after Silver Cloud gave me that feather, I began to notice feathers – everywhere I walked.
When I first noticed the feathers, I said, wryly, to myself: "Oh, Silver Cloud must have been down here, he's dropped a feather". However, I soon saw these

feathers as a sign that I was "going the right way" and was "on the right path" – the reason being, for instance, I would see a feather, on the ground. - outside a shop I intended to visit.

I also found the feathers after I had made a decision about something – they were a confirmation, a sign that my guides were with me - or - usually - several steps ahead of me.

I still acknowledge the feathers that I see, as I go along my path.

27th September 1994.

Did vibrations.
I saw the younger Silver Cloud.
Silver Cloud, Buffalo and myself sat in my "place" for a while.
I told them both, that I really value these moments.
Silver Cloud said that he had some preparation work to do.
I left.

My feather is still there.

28th September 1994.

2pm: Did vibrations. Felt them lift. Saw nothing.

3.15pm: Did vibrations. Saw Buffalo and Silver Cloud. I asked if Kato would give any communication:

"He has a lot to say. He will start soon".

"Keep asking for the highest order".

28th September 1994.

Silver Cloud likened my "place" to a railway station from which lines ran outwards in many directions, an image, which I could see in my head, as he spoke.
The lines, were the communication lines, on which I travelled when I tuned to a visiting Spirit.

"Always return to the station" he said, *"then we know where you are".*

"The chakras are the link between the physical and the spiritual – you are breathing in a life force – not only to sustain your own physical well being – but breathing in the life force of the world which is beyond".

"Meditation is important – to meditate for a few minutes a day is most valuable because you are breathing in the life force".

"This should be done as a daily exercise"

"Come back later".

Later that evening, and with John present, I returned to my "place" and saw that Kato was there.
Kato said *"Good evening"* and Silver Cloud said *"Tell John to ask his questions".*

At the end of a lengthy communication, in which Kato answered questions regarding various patients that John was seeing – Kato said:

"We have used our allotted time – it has been interesting".

219

Silver Cloud said;

"You will find the question and answers will be very beneficial".

Then,

"You may go. A better performance – 7/10".

Before I left I said to Silver Cloud;

"You'll leave my feather there, won't you?"

To which came the reply;

"I'm surprised it hasn't blown away, the way you breeze in and out!"

I returned to my chair.
Returning to my chair allowed me to relax and clear the energy of the last communication, it allowed John and I to discuss the communication if we wanted to, and, it was a further opportunity to have another cup of tea and a cigarette for me.
Clearing the energy is a very important exercise for me, as this allows me, to not only clear my energy field, but my mind – ready to give total concentration to the next Spirit.
Also – maintaining the vibration for a length of time takes practice.

Silver Cloud understood my need to "return to my chair" and would send me back to it – BUT not dismiss me. I was therefore, always "listening", and remained sensitive to his descending energy in order that I did not miss my cue to return.

The cue came, for me to return to my "place:"

On my return, I found Mr Bennett eager to communicate with John, and to answer his questions relating to one patient in particular. As the communication came to a close Mr Bennett said:

"I have worked with other healers – but I think I will stay here".

"Of course – Kato is a gentleman and Laura – well, she is a fine young lady – a little on the flippant side".

"I am so pleased to be able to speak directly to you and I shall enjoy visiting again".

"Well, I shall take my leave – Good Evening".

During the last month or so, not only had I met John's guides, but also, I had been introduced to two other guides.
One was the guide of a healer friend – the other – the guide of our dowser friend, Stan.
It was brilliant to meet all these people and to receive and pass on, their communication. I felt privileged to work for them and the reaction of our two friends, after they had received their communication, made me feel as though I was doing a worthwhile job.
I felt very comfortable under the protection and guidance of Buffalo and Silver Cloud and felt very secure in the system of working that they had set up for me.

3rd October 1994 10pm ish.

Raised vibrations.

I felt like I was climbing up a ladder although I could not see one, it took more effort to reach my "place".
When I got to my "place" Buffalo said;
"Hooray! – We've moved up one".
"This will cure your vertigo".
"We've been waiting for you".

I was feeling the effect of my higher vibrations, there was a great deal of energy around and within me. I needed to ground myself – but it was my Spirit that was up there, my body was a long way away?
Continuing, Buffalo said;

"We need to be higher – to afford more protection for you".

"You will remember this level".

I could feel my vibrations lowering as Buffalo spoke;

"I'm slipping back down!" I called.

Buffalo immediately grabbed hold of my arms and my vibrations stabilised to a level I could maintain. Then they began to lift again – and then I began to slip back.

Still keeping his grip on me, Buffalo said;

"You are really amongst us now.
You come in through the front door.
The door at the back (of my "place") *is the entrance to the spirit world.*
This room is set aside, within the spirit community – a meeting place. They must stay on their side and you must stay on your side.
A meeting place of the two worlds".

"That is all you need to know for the time being – you got here".

"Return now, to your own world".

Needless to say, on my return to my chair, my vibrations were beating fast, as was my heart. It took much grounding on my part, to quieten the vibrations.

4th October 1994.

Raised vibrations.
Eventually I saw the bottom rung of an aluminium ladder.
I climbed up the ladder – no one there – just empty space.
Repeatedly asked for Buffalo's help – there was no reply.
After 1 hour – I stopped trying.

I climbed that ladder over a period of days and nights.
I never knew if I would reach my "place" or where my place would be. They appeared to be moving it.
However, when Stan, the dowser, asked me if he could come to receive communication from his guide - I found my "place" and his waiting guide – with ease.

At other attempts, notably, those occasions when I was just visiting - my "place" had moved up.

I well remember one occasion, when, as I was struggling to reach the top of the ladder to step off into my place – the effort was becoming too great.
As I wearily climbed that ladder I was calling for Buffalo to help me.

Just as I thought I would slip back, Buffalo's' hands appeared out of the mist which swirled above me.
He reached down, and I grasped both his hands.
He held on, and I climbed.
On reaching the topmost rung of the ladder, I stepped of it and into the safe haven of my place and of Buffalo.

17th October 1994.

Went to my "place".
I couldn't see anyone there, but I noticed how cold it was.
Standing in the cold, I sensed the vibration of White Cloud. (Silver Clouds' guide)
I asked Buffalo to come.
Buffalo appeared and began to speak; I realised that his words, were the words of White Cloud.
Buffalo was channelling White Cloud.
The words he spoke were:

"We wished to move to a higher level – the higher level will make it easier for us to protect you and ourselves".

"As we have moved to this higher level – I have become involved in your work".

"You must go".

I returned to my chair, my heart beating fast.
I returned to ponder on White Clouds' words.
I returned – and wondered, "What next?"

CHAPTER FOURTEEN

GOODBYE and THANKYOU.

And so I bring this part of my story to an end. Little did I realise, that within a month, Buffalo would move on:

Move on to be a guide.

Some fortunate channel would soon be full of excitement and anticipation as they met him, eager to work with him – keen to learn about him – grow to love him - as I will always love him, and, be very grateful to him.

I would be given prior warning of this event.

I would be told that Buffalo was "training" another doorkeeper.

I would be told that Buffalo would choose the time of his leaving.

I would continue to work, during this uncertain time.

On the 11th November 1994 – I would meet Wolf.

My learning had only just begun.

I would continue to work with Silver Cloud, and meet with more challenges along the way. I would continue in my efforts to attune to the "Highest order" and I would embark on an amazing journey to America.

In fact, I worked with the American Indian energies for a further 7 years.

Then in September 2001, I met a new guide whose name is Salamander – a Palestinian Healer.

In the summer of 2006 Salamander moved on, and a Native American guide returned – His name is Red Cloud.

Looking back at those times I have written about - when I received that communication, saw and experienced those amazing things, and met those incredible people – I vowed that I would never forget any of them.

It wasn't until I began to read through my notebooks, that I realised that I had forgotten an awful lot of details. Thank heaven, I wrote them all down!

In the beginning, having decided that I must write this book – I said to my guides and helpers: "Right   - I know where this book starts - where do I finish it?"

The reply came:

"Finish with the ladder".

In September 2006 - as I was ¾ of the way through chapter 13, with its,' ladder story – Amos, an ancient prophet and a much loved and valued guide, suddenly said to me, as I was putting the kettle on:

"Spirits In The Sky" – that's the title of the second book".

"What – Pardon - I've got to do another, I haven't finished this one yet!"
My mind immediately raced through all those events still confined to my notebooks – at least, the ones that I remembered.

Three or four nights later, as I raised vibrations, I found Buffalo, Wolf, Silver Cloud and White Cloud all standing together in a line, in my "place". Red Cloud was with them.

Silver Cloud said:

"We all want to be in the same book".

White Cloud added:

"We ARE your "Spirits in the sky".

I was thrilled, not, just to see them all standing together, but - to feel the power of their combined energies was truly awesome.
I love all these people, they are part of me – part of who I am.

They are indeed – my Spirits in the sky.

Returning to my chair, I thought back to the day when Amos had given me the title of the second book – "What day was it? – (I must make a note of it) – I think it was Monday – Monday the 18th, Dads birthday!"
The next day, John confirmed to me that it had indeed been Monday the 18th - (In my excitement, I had telephoned him with my news).

The brilliant revelation for me was, that, twelve years ago, on the 18th September 1994 - my Dad's birthday - Silver Cloud had mentioned to me, for my second time of hearing, the title – "More Friends Than You Know". Now, some 12yrs later, on the same date – I am given another title.

I think it's absolutely brilliant, that Spirit play these meaningful "games" with us – absolutely brilliant!

This time, I will not wait for 12years to pass by before I begin to write – therefore – my given task completed - I will end now.

I have really enjoyed the time that I have spent in writing this book – giving me the opportunity to re-visit my memories and experiences. And I hope that in sharing these things with you, you too, have enjoyed yourselves.
To all of you, on your own spiritual journey of discovery, with its ups and downs, its light and dark – I will leave you with the words of Peter Joseph:

"Positive energy at ALL times!"

And the words of Silver Cloud:

"Have faith – enjoy every small delight and the burden will lift.
I know this to be true – Believe".

For the time being:

Goodbye and Thankyou.

Lynn.

Lynn's Photo Album

A Few Photo's relevant to the words in this book

You'll find some of the dogs, people and places etc.........

Mum -
my Sister
and
Laddie.
before
I was born

Me -
aged 8 or 9
months.
I'm smiling
because Mum
has taken off
my straps

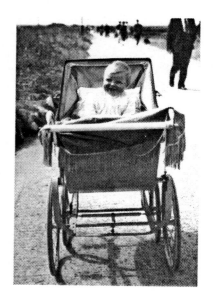

Me With Teddy

Aged around 2 yrs with "Teddy" - the present
from Grandaddad Jack

My Sister giving me a helping hand

Me - aged 5 or 6

Mum and Dad in the garden of the
"ex-rectory" we moved into.
In the background is the Church

Me and my friend Moss

If you look carefully you will see me in the apex
of the Apple tree - Moss is "mooching"

Me and Shep taking in
the sun
(about 1967)

An elderly Shep,
pottering in the field
at the rear of the
house

We've alwys liked this
photograph of John
and I - taken in 1969

Approximately 18 years
later I took my driving
test and passed on the
4th attempt!

Portsmouth Harbour - pleasure trip - early 70's

On Honeymoon at Conway Castle - March 1974

Trampas
at about 4 months old

Muppet
approx 3 months old

The picture that lived in the airing cupboard

"Positve Energy at All Times"

"Great Grandfather" - Peter Joseph
"Great Grandmother" - Dinah

Grandmother
&
Peter Joseph

Granddad William
"Taking 5 Minutes"

Uncle Arthur
The writer of the
"Birth Congratulations"
card

Armon on the day of
his wedding to
Dorothy

Granddad William on his coal round

Granddad "Jack" and Grandma
with my sister
(who knew Granddad as Grandpa)

Mum and Dad

This is the last picture I have of
Mum and Dad

My In-Laws

This photograph always
makes John and I smile.
It shows Elise's sunny
character

A happy, relaxed
John

Me and Trampas
A Favourite picture of mine

Muppet
His nose could resemble
a bottle cleaner

Trampas
Shows his appealing
blue eyes

Trampas and Muppet

A Grooming Challenge !

Trampas
"Be Careful Trampas
Don't knock them over "

Muppet
Aged about 13 yrs

The joke Dad and I were sharing was
The Vicar had forgotten to Turn-Up *(Honest !)*

With the Vicar found and the vows taken
John and I sign the register

I was fortunate enough to be able to
go with John when he went to photograph the
great steeplechaser Red Rum

Post Script

Do you remember, in Chapter 2,
I couldn't find that Mcguiness Flint
record - neither could I remember
it's title

- WELL -

In response to my periodic
mumblings of dis-satisfaction, John
did a "search" on the internet.

I can now reveal - the title is:

"When I'm Dead and Gone"

How cool is that! Talk about omens
for the future. It even has the name
"John" in one of the verses.
BRILLIANT!

P.P.S - I'm must go now - the tune is
running through my head and I've
just thought of a cardboard box that I
haven't looked in yet!

Bye.

Up to date information about Lynn and
her other publications can be found on her
website:

www.GoldenCloud.co.uk

Printed in the United Kingdom
by Lightning Source UK Ltd.
119067UK00001BA/1-48

9 780953 494637